MADE TO GROW CALLED TO GO

Your Road Trip for Spiritual Transformation,
One Mile at a Time

T.C. Chang

Made to Grow Called to Go: Your Road Trip for Spiritual Transformation, One Mile at a Time

Copyright © 2025 by T.C. Chang

ISBN: 979-8-218-71922-7 (paperback)

All sources are marked by superscript numbers (for example [1,2,3] ...) and can be found on page 103 in the *Sources Used* section at the end of the book.

To contact me or invite me to speak, please go to: www.tc-chang-official.com

TABLE OF CONTENTS

Acknowledgements

This book would not exist without the love and support of some very important people in my life.

To my wife – thank you for being my steady place, my sounding board, my counterbalance, and my greatest encourager. Your belief in me has meant more than I can ever express. I'm endlessly grateful for your patience, prayer, and partnership. I look forward to many more years of adventures, talking me out of rash decisions, and bowls of chips-n-salsa,

To my kids – you remind me every day why the JOURNEY matters. Your wonder, silliness, and love inspire me to keep growing every day. Since you are the legacy I care most about, every sentence in this book is written with you in mind. I hope this book points you toward a faith that is real and a life that is full.

To my parents – I'm deeply grateful for the foundation you gave me. Your discipline, conviction, and commitment to the humble truth were guardrails that kept my feet from slipping too far. I see it now: the narrow road you held to was a lifeline and it helped lead me here.

My closest friends – thank you for sticking nearby through the real and the raw. For the long talks, the trips, the honesty, the prayers, the food, and the laughter. You've helped shape not just this book, but my life. OGs/Diamonds/KFT/Gilberts

To all who've walked with me – your impact runs through every chapter. I'm grateful beyond words.

INTRODUCTION

If you've picked up this book, I am hoping it means you've heard the call—the same call that Jesus gave His followers more than two thousand years ago. The Great Commission: to go, make disciples of all nations, baptizing and teaching them to obey everything He commanded (*Matthew 28:19-20*). This isn't just a suggestion; it's the heartbeat of every believer's journey.

Growth in Christ is not merely about personal improvement or about the increase in spiritual comfort. It's about preparing you to live on mission—fully equipped, fully alive, and fully ready to share the love and truth of Jesus with a world desperately in need of hope. The road of spiritual growth is the training ground for the Great Commission, the path that leads you deeper into God's purpose and power.

My question to you is: Do you believe you've fully grown in godly wisdom and stature, with favor with God and man (as Jesus is referenced in Luke chapter 2)?

If your answer is **YES**, then move on, put the book down, and put on your crown of glory—because you, my friend, have already overcome!

If your answer is **NO**—which I assumed would be your response—then please know that this book **is** for you.

The greatest threat to our walk of faith is the false confidence that we've already made it. The Apostle Paul wrote:

> *Not that I have already obtained all this, or have already arrived at my goal, but I press on to take hold of that for which Christ Jesus took hold of me. (Philippians 3:12 NIV)*

That is, in fact, one of the most dangerous religious mindsets to possess. It's in that very moment—when you let your guard down—that you are blindsided and find yourself on a fast track in reverse, before you even realize it.

This book is an invitation to go on a journey. This journey will stretch you. It will challenge your habits, your heart, and your priorities. You will encounter seasons of breakthrough and seasons that test your faith. But through it all, God's hand is guiding you, shaping you, and preparing you to be a disciple who makes other disciples.

Inside this book, you'll find practical tools implemented in the real world, rooted in Scripture, designed to help you clear away distractions, organize your life around God's priorities, shine with His presence, and sustain a lifestyle of faithful obedience. These tools aren't just checklists to tick off nor are they work-based steps to get closer to God. Rather, the tools and methods I reference are invitations to live a life marked by intentional growth so you can fulfill your calling with confidence and love.

Spiritual growth is not about following a formula. It is about a relationship—with Jesus, the Savior and the Way. As you walk with Him, He empowers you by His Spirit to be transformed and to transform those around you. The journey isn't about arriving at perfection but about continuing forward with purpose until the day He returns.

So, as you read these pages, be aware that your growth fuels the mission. Whether you're at the beginning of this journey or well down the road, remember this: God is not finished with you yet. He is constantly unfolding new landscapes, casting fresh vision, and inviting you to join Him even deeper in the work of making disciples. There's always more road—more growth, more purpose, more mission. And with every step, He's drawing you closer to Himself and sending you farther into the world.

Because in the Kingdom of God, the call is clear: grow deep, go far, and make disciples. As such, there's always more road ahead.

CHAPTER 1

FUNDAMENTALS

I'm an avid motorcycle rider; my wife definitely hates that. When I first learned to ride, I took a beginner motorcycle course offered through the state's Bureau of Motor Vehicles. The first day of classes was spent entirely in a classroom—with booklets, slides, and a couple of instructors speaking about the topic of riding.

After that first day, despite the details they provided, the verbal cautions, and the abundance of vivid pictures, I was not yet ready to fully step into the role of a motorcycle rider. It was just head knowledge at this point.

The subsequent days were spent outdoors in a closed parking lot filled with orange cones. I, along with a cohort of 15 other strangers, spent days learning how to use the basic functions of the equipment, as well as dozens of habits to begin developing as a rider—checking mirrors, turning heads, braking with both front and rear brakes, looking through and past a turn, to name a few.

But even after the rigor of practicing these habits, I still couldn't call myself a motorcyclist.

Many of these tools and habits were just sets of arbitrary actions and didn't bring any real value yet. It wasn't until after the class series was completed, and I had spent time on the open road—interacting with other drivers and deploying these actions enough to develop real habits—that I began to feel like I was advancing as a rider.

In the real world, these very actions-turned-habits are the difference between safety and risk, life and death. In like manner, this book serves as a guide to deepen your Christian experience—not a step-by-step instruction manual to Jesus. The guidance in this book is designed to help you create habits.

We know that habits themselves don't equate to personally knowing Jesus, but they *can* be the difference between actions resulting in life or actions resulting in death. Yes, lots of suspense here.

Over the past decade and a half, I've had the pleasure of helping businesses—large and small—get closer to their aspirational goals for profit, revenue, market share, and long-term transformation. Regardless of the size, industry, or team makeup, one thing is consistent in all of these clients: big-picture outcomes are the byproduct of detailed processes.

By trade, I am an expert in refining processes, looking for opportunities to create more efficient ones, and helping the individuals who perform the work solve their own problems. I hold a certification in Lean Six Sigma as a Black Belt, having spent hundreds—if not thousands—of hours with frontline employees of some very large Fortune companies, helping teams figure out how to perform more effectively.

As a baseline, since you may or may not be familiar, Lean Six Sima is a method for improving how work gets done in an organization. It combines two powerful ideas:

- Lean, which focuses on removing 'waste' and making processes flow more smoothly, and
- Six Sigma, which focuses on reducing errors and improving quality by using data and problem-solving tools.

Together, Lean Six Sigma helps teams work faster, smarter, and more efficiently – delivering better results with less frustration.

A Lean Six Sigma Black Belt is someone who has been trained to lead improvement efforts using this approach. Black Belts know how to analyze data, find root causes of problems, guide leaders and teams alike toward practical, lasting solutions. Given the name Black Belt, think of them as process ninjas! There are also White Belts, Yellow Belts, Green Belts, Black Belts, and even Master Black Belts, each requiring a set of training and each level possessing an incrementally stronger ability to practice, train, and execute the principles and tools of Lean Six Sigma.

In the years that I have spent working with organizations, a recurring conundrum seems to always surface: the minutiae of procedures can often be buried by complexity, bureaucracy, and competing priorities. Yet at the same time, no organization can thrive over time unless it has a structured approach to managing its day-to-day activities. Is there a world where this paradox isn't a harsh reality?

Have you ever watched a crew team perform? The goal is obvious—get your boat (technically called a "shell") to cross a particular distance and reach the finish line first.

Can you imagine a shell filled with rowers who row at their own pace, with zero coordination, and varying degrees of urgency? I'd call it a miracle if they traveled in a straight line, let alone finished with a competitive time.

Unfortunately, many organizations don't give enough focused attention to the details of what their team members are doing— like rowing in sync to a certain rhythm, using the same motions to maximize weight distribution, or even how and where their hands should grip the oar.

Despite common misconception, this is not micromanagement (which carries a disrespectful connotation); rather, it's about setting people up for success. When you perfect the details, create structured norms, and align employees to purpose, success—however that is defined—is an inevitable outcome.

When it comes to your individual growth in God, the same principles that help global companies thrive can be applied at a personal level to propel you deeper into your experiential knowledge of Him.

It all starts with the fundamentals.

Years ago, my son played soccer with the grandson of the great Bo Schembechler—whose nickname (you guessed it) was also Bo. Being one of the team's coaches, I often found myself reminded of one of the greatest principles that big Bo brought to the game of football (or sports in general): *Never lose focus on the fundamentals.*

There are fabled stories of Coach Bo bringing his players together during halftime of a heated game, holding up a football, and asking his players what he was holding in his hands. Some would call this degrading or menial. Bo called it *focusing on the fundamentals*[1].

He believed that even advanced strategies and tactics were built upon a solid foundation of blocking, tackling, and other fundamental football skills. The point he was trying to make was that unless you maintain a continual grasp of the basics, you can never advance.

And if you never advance, your goals will never be attained. He may have been onto something—with a career record of 234 wins, 65 losses, and 8 ties.

Through this book, my hope is to help you grasp the fundamentals—and never lose sight of them—even as you grow, advance, and mature. As you install the necessary building blocks in your own life, you're creating a structure that allows God to increase His advancement, growth, and maturity in you so you can become an even more effective disciple.

This is a road trip, and you're in the driver's seat. Think of me as your mechanic, here to ensure your systems are stable and can carry you the distance.

Like any transformation—whether personal or business—the journey will take time. When I spend time at client sites, I don't guarantee overnight transformation. I can't.

True transformation isn't just mimicking a set of unfamiliar actions or reciting borrowed lingo. True transformation is metamorphosis—a fundamental change in constitution and makeup.

And we all, who with unveiled faces contemplate the Lord's glory, are being transformed into his image with ever-increasing glory, which comes from the Lord, who is the Spirit. (2 Corinthians 3:18 NIV)

When employees in organizations start to THINK differently, it organically leads to a change in how they PERFORM—that's true transformation.

When leaders take a step back and begin using the right motivational tools to develop others as leaders—that's true transformation.

It takes time. Habits can be put in place within weeks, but it takes months—if not years—for fruit to be evident. And as maturity sets in, one would expect to produce exponential yields. The same holds true for spiritual transformation. Yes, we absolutely can have dynamic experiences where God miraculously changes our thoughts, gives us clarity, and heals what's broken—inside and out. But if we don't have personal structure in our lives to support continued growth, we are apt to slide backward and miss the fullness of His work.

Spiritual growth takes time, just like a meaningful road trip.

CHAPTER 2

THE NEED TO TRAVEL

This physical world as we know it is vast—so large, and there's so much to see. Just one country alone holds endless sights and experiences, let alone an entire planet. I'm always surprised when I meet people who have never left their state—some, not even their county. I mean, Ohio is nice (*mild sarcasm here*), but have you seen the state of Washington? Beautiful (*no sarcasm*)!

Meeting different cultures, eating new foods, hearing different accents, and exploring unfamiliar landmarks is exactly why people travel. These experiences expand our perspective and stretch our understanding of life beyond our own zip code.

Before the internet and the flood of media now at our fingertips, people simply didn't know what was out there. The urge to explore wasn't natural to most. A person born and raised in a quiet Indiana farm town might never realize that a trip to the Grand Canyon could literally change their life. Someone growing up in the deserts of Arizona might never imagine the power of standing before the vast, crashing waves of the Atlantic. But today, with access to endless stories and snapshots from around the globe, we're exposed to more than ever— dreaming, planning, and hoping for adventures that once seemed unreachable. I can't go a day without my wife sending me videos of Aruba, Bali, Fiji, Maldives, and other destinations I don't know how to pronounce or spell.

Spiritually speaking, many Christians are stuck in their own faith bubble. They only know the version of God they grew up with, or the one they've constructed from a limited understanding of Scripture. They don't realize that there's so much more to discover.

> *Oh, the depth of the riches and wisdom and knowledge of God! How unsearchable are his judgments and how inscrutable his ways! (Romans 11:33 ESV)*

They're innocently unaware that there's an entire world of exciting, life-altering experiences with God waiting for them—if they would only dare to venture out. But you can't desire a destination you don't even know exists.

That's why standards matter.

Standards Create Need

One of the most common phrases I hear on job sites is, "I wasn't shown how to do it—I just figured it out and made it work." You've probably lived that yourself at some point. It's frustrating and discouraging when you're left to guess your way through something important.

The problem isn't with the person—it's with the lack of clarity.

The same holds true in our spiritual lives. Thankfully, God doesn't leave us fumbling in the dark. He doesn't expect us to piece things together and hope it somehow works. He gave us a standard. He gave us Jesus.

Those who say they live in God should live their
lives as Jesus did. (1 John 2:6 NLT)

Jesus didn't just come to pay for our sin. He came to model what full alignment with God looks like—what humanity joined with divinity can do. He is the gold standard, the divine SOP (Standard Operating Procedure) fully fleshed out. And the Bible given to us as our training manual.

But let's pause here—because I've had leaders tell me that setting standards for employees is insulting. They argue that it demoralizes employees or limits creativity. I get the heart behind that sentiment. But when I hear it, I always ask one question: Do you care enough about your employees to want them to still have a job five years from now?

The answer is always yes.

That's when I explain the difference between controlling and equipping. Standards don't restrict people—they empower them. They create a target to aim for and give people something solid to measure against. Without a standard, you'll never objectively know that you're off-track. Without being able to identify the gaps, there's no opportunity for growth.

In the corporate world, this is why Six Sigma exists. The goal isn't literal perfection—it's pursuing excellence. In Six Sigma methodology, a process that yields only 3.4 defects per million times that you attempt it is considered to have 'world-class' quality, or Six Sigma[2]. That's a success rate of 99.99966%. Organizations pursue that benchmark not because they expect perfection, but because it drives progress.

Jesus is our Six Sigma. We may never hit 100%—but striving for that image, becoming more like Him day by day, that's the goal.

For God knew his people in advance, and he chose them to become like his Son, so that his Son would be the firstborn among many brothers and sisters. (Romans 8:29 NLT)

So all of us who have had that veil removed can see and reflect the glory of the Lord. And the Lord— who is the Spirit—makes us more and more like him as we are changed into his glorious image. (2 Corinthians 3:18 NLT)

Transformation doesn't happen overnight. It happens by proximity. Like a mirror reflects what's in front of it, our lives begin to reflect Christ the longer we stay close to Him. We'll dig into the *how* later in this book—but for now, know that transformation is less about performance and more about presence.

And here's where it all ties back to the road trip.

You'll never know you're not moving if you don't check the map. And you'll never arrive anywhere new if you don't recognize where you're starting from. Jesus isn't using your missed targets to condemn you—He's using them to coach you.

Therefore there is now no condemnation [no guilty verdict, no punishment] for those who are in Christ Jesus [who believe in Him as personal Lord and Savior]. (Romans 8:1 AMP)

God is not the cruel boss waiting to punish your every mistake. He's the loving Father who wants to equip you for the journey ahead. In fact, He is yearning for you to stumble into the desire of wanting more. The question is: will you choose to take what He's given and start moving forward—or will you stay stuck in what's comfortable, familiar, and unchallenged?

> *... I have set before you life and death, blessings and curses. Now choose life, so that you and your children may live. (Deuteronomy 30:19b NIV)*

So why do we need to travel? Because staying put guarantees spiritual stagnation. This chapter isn't just about exploring exotic lands or chasing a metaphor—it's about recognizing that transformation requires movement. Standards don't imprison us; they invite us. And Jesus, our flawless example, beckons us forward—not with shame, but with grace and possibility.

You were never meant to "just make it work." You were made to *grow*, to *move*, to *be transformed*. The question isn't whether the journey is available. It's whether you're willing to leave your driveway.

CHAPTER 3

ROADMAP & DIRECTIONS

Every legitimate journey has a destination. I've heard it said that sometimes the journey *is* the destination — well, to me that's called being nomadic. The definition of a true journey is the act of traveling from one place to another. When you are trying to get to a specific destination, you kind of have to know where you are going (*stating the obvious here*). If nothing else, you need to know which direction you are heading.

The same can be said about your own spiritual journey. Is it intentional? Or do you find yourself just "going for a drive" and hoping that you end up somewhere good? My opinion is that life is too short and your spiritual health is too important for such casualness to dictate the path that you take.

> *Look carefully then how you walk, not as unwise but as wise, making the best use of the time, because the days are evil. Therefore do not be foolish, but understand what the will of the Lord is. (Ephesians 5:15-17 ESV)*

So where are you headed? Have you ever thought about that? It's okay if you haven't; having awareness of this concept is an excellent starting point. Sure, you know that the destination is ultimately Jesus — but that's awfully vague, isn't it?

Generically, one could declare that the direction that every business is ideally moving in is the one that generates profit. That's a no-brainer, duh. The direction I'm referring to here is much more specific. It is more along the lines of targeted goals and milestones.

Many businesses that I interact with tend to fall into one of two camps — they either are so focused on where they are going (*strategy*) that they pay little attention to the mechanics of how to execute, or they are so focused on the details of day-to-day execution that they miss the forest for the trees (*no strategy*).

Both contain a severe and innate threat to their own business continuity, but when an organization does not possess a roadmap for where they're headed, momentum will most definitely stall, leaving its constituents (*employees*) flapping like mad, yet going nowhere. In scenarios like this, before even thinking about processes, systems, or infrastructure, I call a time-out and ensure there is sound strategy before we do anything else.

This is where Hoshin Kanri comes into the picture.

What is Hoshin Kanri? It's Japanese! Bet you didn't know that you would be getting Japanese language lessons as part of reading this book, did you? Eh, that's what I call fringe benefits! Throughout this book, I will be introducing various tools that I consistently use in my line of work, many of which have Japanese names. Incidentally, my last name is Chang, which is not Japanese, so my use of Japanese concepts has nothing to do with my ethnic (*Taiwanese*) background. Just getting that out of the way.

Many of the principles, tools, and methodologies that I regularly utilize happen to have some very deep roots in the automotive production environment of the '30s and '40s.

One of the key innovators of Lean practices and Lean thinking was Toyota[3], an overseas car manufacturer that was eventually able to leapfrog every major domestic automotive manufacturer on the market. Remember, Lean is the strategic focus on removing waste from processes.

How did Toyota do it? It certainly was not luck or timing. It was solely due to the transformative thinking that they were able to implement, which enabled them to make cars cheaper, faster, and of better quality. They developed and mastered workforce tools and concepts and created an operational model to empower employees, which was drastically different from every other competitor in their industry.

In 1986, the movie *Gung Ho*, starring Michael Keaton, captured the emotions behind some of these differences when Japanese automotive manufacturing was introduced to a traditional manufacturing plant.

Fast forward nearly a century, and we find that many, if not most, of these same methods are now universally applicable to all types of industries, in all segments of the workforce.

Hoshin is loosely translated as "compass needle" or "direction," and Kanri is translated to mean "execution" or "delivery." The concept of Hoshin Kanri[4] is quite commonsensical and fundamental, yet few actually put it in regular practice.

Simply put, strategy and direction have to be set, and then action needs to be "deployed" or executed at all levels of an organization to make progress a reality. Let's frame it a different way.

A goal WITHOUT a deadline is called a fantasy.

A goal WITH a deadline is called an objective.

A goal with a deadline AND a plan is called an intent.

A goal with a deadline, a plan, AND consistent action is called success.

Bottom line is this: meaningful goals with a deadlines, plans, and consistent actions is called *fulfillment*.

This is what Hoshin Kanri helps to deliver — fulfillment. There are five steps or elements to completing Hoshin Kanri:

- Breakthrough Goals
- Annual Goals
- Actions and Initiatives
- Measurements
- Accountability

Let's dive into each one of these in more detail.

Breakthrough Goals

What did you want to be when you were growing up? Soccer player? Doctor? A Lean Six Sigma Black Belt? Hah, no one ever names that one as a kid! For most of us, we weren't exactly sure what we wanted to be when we grew up. We may have had certain inclinations or preferences, but that perhaps changed every few years, depending on our experiences and environment. For some people, a smaller subset of the population, they knew exactly what they wanted to be.

LeBron James knew as a young child that his goal was to be a professional basketball player. If you follow his life story, you will see that at every turn, his decisions were made based on that chartered direction. The habits that he established were based on the destiny that he saw for himself. The sacrifices he made were for the sake of attaining his goal. Being an elite professional basketball player was his goal, his breakthrough objective, and he never deviated, never changed direction, never lost sight of that targeted goal.

In the business world, I help organizational leaders determine and etch out their business' future. It's fun and exciting to vision-cast and dream of the possibilities that lie beyond. When I ask leaders what they want their organization to be when it grows up, I help to frame it from multiple perspectives.

What do your customers need you to be in 3–5 years?

What do your employees need you to be in 3–5 years?

What does the industry or market need you to be in 3–5 years?

Oftentimes, this helps them decide upon their vision from a balanced, 360-degree perspective. For some organizations, they want to be best-in-class in their industry. They may want to have the strongest employee engagement, based on Gartner surveys. They may want to hit over $1 billion in revenue or some aspirational number in operating income.

These are goals that are lofty and, frankly, should make leaders uncomfortable. I always say that if you can reach these goals through your current trajectory, then they aren't aggressive enough. These goals are meant to take you from status quo to BREAKTHROUGH — think big! At this stage, forget the "how" and all the associated tactical details; let's keep our heads in the sky so we can see far enough on the horizon.

In your spiritual life, regardless of where you are at right now, what do you want to be when you grow up? In 5 years, do you see yourself answering the call to pastor a church? In 5 years, would you like to be leading a Bible study from your home? In 5 years, are you actively involved in youth ministry? In 5 years, are you fulfilling your calling to lead authentic worship at your local church? In 5 years, are you publishing a book about spiritual growth?

For some of you, there may not be a specific 'role' or function that is associated with this goal. It could be some outcome from faith, a manifestation of God working through you, or some spiritual aspiration that is linked to spiritual growth. Whatever those goals may be, you must still be specific in what you think your outcome should be. As such, let me use the same technique that I use for business leaders to bring a more well-rounded approach to this. To start, ask yourself these questions:

- What does my spouse need me to be in 5 years?
- What do my kids need me to be in 5 years?
- What does my local church need me to be in 5 years?
- What does my community need me to be in 5 years?
- What do my co-workers or neighbors need me to be in 5 years?
- What does my extended family need me to be in 5 years?

Some of these questions may not pertain to you. Some of you already know the answers to these questions. However, many of you have yet to understand how to answer them. Unlike my experiences in business, where you can autonomously set your own destiny (right or wrong), your destiny has already been determined for you.

'For I know the plans I have for you,' declares the LORD, "plans to prosper you and not to harm you, plans to give you hope and a future." Jeremiah 29:11 NIV)

You have not chosen Me, but I have chosen you and I have appointed and placed and purposefully planted you, so that you would go and bear fruit and keep on bearing, and that your fruit will remain and be lasting, so that whatever you ask of the Father in My name [as My representative] He may give to you. (John 15:16 AMP)

The Lord will fulfill his purpose for me; your steadfast love, O Lord, endures forever. Do not forsake the work of your hands. (Psalm 138:8 ESV)

On one hand, it's comforting to know that you don't have to pick the right answer; it kind of takes the pressure off. Yet, on the other hand, it can be difficult to proceed unless you do know the plans that God has for you. Regardless, God has big plans for all of us. His plans are lofty; they are grand; they make us uncomfortable. This is now your opportunity to seek His presence, seek His Word, and seek the answers.

I love those who love me, and those who seek me find me. (Proverbs 8:18 NIV)

Keep on asking, and you will receive what you ask for. Keep on seeking, and you will find. Keep on knocking, and the door will be opened to you. For everyone who asks, receives. Everyone who seeks, finds. And to everyone who knocks, the door will be opened. (Matthew 7:7-8 NLT)

When you simply ask God (out of a pure heart), God is faithful and righteous to answer. He may reveal to you through ministry work. He may have individuals in your life provide you with confirmation. He may speak to you directly through the Word. He may give you dreams and visions. You may hear Him in your spirit-man through a strong discerning sense. Regardless of how (because those are innumerable), God WILL reveal it when you seek it.

One key thing to keep in mind is not to worry about the *how*. As a realist and a process-oriented guy, I am constantly thinking about the specific steps it takes to get from point A to point B. Even I must proactively force myself to turn off that mode of thinking. Right now, just focus on the *what* and *where*. What will you be in 5 years? Where will you be in 5 years on your walk? The *how* comes later in this journey.

Once you have a good idea of where or what God wants you to be in 5 years from today, write it down. Document it. Make it visual! Make it present and in your face! Faith comes by hearing! If faith is the substantiation of things hoped for, then make these goals the things that you're hoping for! Flip to page 111 and complete the rows that are labeled "Breakthrough Goals" to begin documenting your personal spiritual strategy.

Annual Goals

Every well-planned road trip has built-in milestones. If you're planning to go on an 800-mile road trip, you will probably have an idea of where you want to stop for food, gas, or even to see some sights. These milestones not only help us become more planful but also make our trip more interesting and enjoyable. Considering that I call myself a foodie, a large part of any road trip for me is figuring out what and where I want to stop to eat!

I mean, who doesn't enjoy tasting progress throughout the process??

Years ago, I was oddly (aka dumbly) interested in distance running as a hobby. I now chuckle at the word *hobby* used for running. I'm happy to announce that I have since been fully delivered from that mental illness. Sure, 13.1 miles or 26.2 miles was a goal that I had in mind prior to each of these events, but mentally, that is not what I relied on to keep me going mile after mile during the events.

My fuel was not the anticipation of the generous buffet of food often provided at the finish line, nor the satisfying moment of relief when I could finally stop running.

The fuel that kept me going was the intentional action of setting mental markers for when I could allow myself a quick sip of water.

The fuel to keep going was my eyes spotting a specific building or landmark far out on the horizon and making that my temporary next target.

The fuel was my mind telling my legs that we just had to make it over the crest of this next hill. The secret to longevity is successfully hitting near-term targets, sequentially, one after another, repeatedly.

Long-term goals set the direction for your course; short-term goals keep you on track in that direction and help you maintain the pace at which you are traveling.

Setting one-year or shorter-term goals is an effective method to accomplishing both. You can ensure that you're taking baby steps (or leaps and bounds) in the right direction *and* set them aggressively enough to arrive where you want to be sometime in the future, say by year five. When a business leader tells me that one of their Breakthrough goals for their organization is to triple their current sales volume, we work together to set a one-year goal that is realistic yet aggressive enough to require introducing some new ways of doing things.

If tripling sales is lofty for five years, does it make sense to shoot for doubling sales in one year? Logic says no; that's way too aggressive.

If their yearly sales volume was 300 units, and knowing what their five-year goal is, would a goal of 305 units for next year make much sense? Logic also says no; it's not aggressive enough, as they can most likely achieve that without doing anything differently.

Typically, I would look for data and use analytics to help set a one-year goal that is somewhat of a stretch, given their current process capacity. Then, in subsequent years, adjust to increase aggressiveness based on progress made.

Let's just pretend you named as one of your Breakthrough goals to actively lead a network of men's Bible studies. Then, I would say the next logical step is to determine what progress toward that looks like after one year.

What is a bite-size, one-year goal you can set for yourself to keep you on track? Perhaps it's something like reading through the entire Bible once. It could be participating in at least one Bible study to determine what you like and don't like as a participant.

Or perhaps a one-year goal could be performing a profound personal study of one book of the Bible, for the sake of developing tactics on how you would teach and guide through the revelation received.

Much like the breakthrough goals, these are also the *WHAT* or *WHERE* types of questions to ask yourself, still intentionally ignoring the *HOW*. We will get there soon enough — relax and stop asking! For each of your Breakthrough goals, you should have at least one yearly goal associated with it.

Flip to page 111 and complete the rows labeled "Annual Goals" to continue building out your personal Hoshin plan.

Actions & Activities

This is the part that everyone always wants to jump to right out of the gate. When I first started learning to drive a car, the very first thing I wanted to do was start the engine, push the gas down, turn the wheel, and start operating. However, as seasoned drivers, we have gained the wisdom to perform some pre-trip checks.

My son, not too long ago, went through the process of learning to drive, and he often jumped right into trying to drive the car instead of performing some pre-drive due diligence. Preparation for a road trip includes checking your mirrors, fastening your seat belt, looking for check-engine lights, turning on headlights, ensuring there's decent tire pressure — to name a few. Similarly, most people have a bias for action but overlook the importance of basic planning actions.

> *For which of you, desiring to build a tower, does not first sit down and count the cost, whether he has enough to complete it? Otherwise, when he has laid a foundation and is not able to finish, all who see it begin to mock him, saying, 'This man began to build and was*

*not able to finish.' Or what king, going out to encounter
another king in war, will not sit down first and
deliberate whether he is able with ten thousand to meet
him who comes against him with twenty thousand?*
(Luke 14:28-33 ESV)

Do your planning and prepare your fields before
building your house. *(Proverbs 24:27 NLT)*

*The plans of the diligent lead surely to
abundance and advantage, But everyone who acts in
haste comes surely to poverty. (Proverbs 21:5 AMP)*

Now that we have performed some due diligence in being
planful, it's time to determine exactly what needs to be done to
achieve our one-year goals. That's right — just our one-year
goals. Many people give up on the journey because they keep
their eyes on that finish line, which is 26.2 miles away. You, on
the other hand, are going to achieve success by keeping your
eyes (and slightly obsessing) on overcoming the very next hill,
and nothing more.

After businesses determine their one-year goals, we move into
the phase that defines *HOW* they will get there. What specific
projects do they need to launch? What initiatives do they need
to kick off? What areas do they need to improve? What is their
operational model to ensure that organizational structure and
efficient processes are put into place? This is where we begin to
impact the organization's day-to-day activities. This is where the
rubber meets the road.

What will it take for you to achieve your goals by this time next
year? What things will you need to do differently? One of the
easiest methods to identify some of these things is SSC — Start,

Stop, Continue. The bottom line is, you're not where you want to be because of three factors:

- You're not doing something that you ought to be doing *(Start)*

- You are doing something that you ought *not* be doing *(Stop)*

- You haven't been doing the right things long enough, or they are working well, so you need to keep at it *(Continue)*

START

To achieve one-year goals, what do you need to *START* doing...like tomorrow? What habits do you need to start forming in your day-to-day? What activities do you need to *start* engaging in?

If one of your goals was to join a worship team, then you're going to want to start doing things like vocal training sessions, looking into audition criteria, or refining your process of getting to a certain skill or aptitude level.

If your goal was to read through the Bible in a year, then you're going to want to start carving out dedicated time every day to read it.

This is your chance to stimulate and initiate the act of *doing* something you haven't done before. We all know that when we continue doing the same things, keeping the same habits, and staying within our comfort zone, we will continue to repeat history over and over, reaping the same results. It goes without saying (but I'll say it anyway) — you'll never get to where you want to go unless you start doing something different.

STOP

What about some of the things you are currently doing — ways you are spending your time, specific activities — that you need to *STOP* doing? This concept often makes people the most uncomfortable. The most obvious are activities and habits that you know are bad for you. These are no-brainers, like drugs and alcohol, porn, and other destructive addictions. Obviously, sin will always be a limiting factor to growth because it separates us from the One who causes growth.

> *But your iniquities have separated you from your God; your sins have hidden his face from you, so that he will not hear. (Isaiah 59:2 NIV)*

They could also be more subtle activities (still sin) like gossiping, lusting, overeating, or movies and media that don't edify your mind or body. However, I challenge you to peel the onion a few layers deeper (and yes, there may be tears). The intent of Hoshin Kanri (if you've forgotten, refer back to page 25) is to build a personal infrastructure that helps you know where you want to go and aids in keeping yourself on track.

How often do you find yourself with great goals but are unable to meet them? What are some of the things that possibly sidetrack you, stealing your time and attention from what is mission-critical?

Too often, I see business leaders who lay out clear and very well-defined strategies but don't understand the importance of removing the activities that hinder their employees from focusing. Or I witness employees who have not been empowered to self-manage their workload, aligning their day-to-day work to the strategy laid out for them.

The radical way to think about it is: you have a handful of goals, right? If the activities and things in which you spend time do not contribute to any of your goals, then that can be an indicator to *stop* doing them. If your goal is to get through the Bible in one year and you have failed in your last seven attempts, do you think the time you spend playing video games or doom scrolling through Instagram helps you toward that goal? I don't think so. If anything, it's working against you.

Find the things in your life that are leeching time, money, and energy. Stop them. Then reallocate those valuable assets toward your identified goals. You will find so much more satisfaction in seeing yourself get closer and closer to meeting your personal growth goals.

CONTINUE

The last area, as mentioned previously, is to *CONTINUE* doing the things that are going well. It's impossible that everything in your life is wrong. Find the positive habits and activities and keep your foot on the gas. Pedal to the metal, baby! Dedicate time to identify and evaluate which activities continue to show positive results — I mean, it's true: if something is working, don't stop!

Find the things that are working and keep doing them. What do you want to continue that will help you achieve your goals? What has been working well up until now, and how can you keep it going?

Flip to page 112 and complete the rows labeled "Actions and Activities" to begin documenting your personal Hoshin plan. If it helps, start with documenting things that you would like to *start, stop,* and *continue.*

Measurements

If only more people spent more time measuring. That's my one plea to humanity. Let me explain — my logic is simple.

When you're driving a car, you won't reach your destination unless you know a few key things:

- Where you're starting from

- Where you want to go

- How to measure your progress along the way

As a long-time Ohioan, I know the distance from Cincinnati to Columbus is 110 miles. On the drive from Columbus to Cincinnati, you'll notice signs every 15-20 miles telling you how far Cincinnati is. Every mile, there's a smaller sign with the highway mile number, so you can track where you are on the road.

Imagine if suddenly you started seeing signs for Cleveland while aiming for Cincinnati. You'd probably pull over somewhere safe, figure out where you went wrong, and get back on track. Without these signs—and without paying attention to them—you might end up like Lloyd in *Dumb and Dumber*, driving miles in the wrong direction.

Besides road signs, your car has an electronic compass showing you which way you're headed, and a speedometer indicating your speed. The speedometer has two functions:

1. It helps you stay within legal speed limits.

2. Second, it helps you calculate when you'll arrive. For example, to get to Cincinnati in two hours, you need to

maintain about 55 mph. If you want to arrive in an hour and a half, you need to average about 73 mph.

Using the speedometer to measure how fast you're moving toward your destination is invaluable if you have a deadline.

In your life, as you pursue goals you've identified, do you have ways to keep yourself on track? What signs tell you that you're progressing, stuck, or off course? What signals tell you if you're moving at the right pace?

Fact: God measures. Throughout scripture, He gives specific measurements and numbers. There's a whole book called *Numbers*. The Ark of the Covenant and Noah's Ark had exact dimensions. Daniel's parables often used specific numbers.

It's no surprise that God desires precision in our pursuit of Him. Our growth and progress should be intentional.

> *The LORD demands accurate scales and balances;*
> *he sets the standards for fairness. (Proverbs 16:11*
> *NLT)*

You might ask, *How do you measure spiritual growth?*

I get that question a lot. It's like in business, where some believe you can't measure what people do, treating employees like "snowflakes" who are exceptions to all rules.

The truth? Most people just measure the wrong things. It's simple: *what gets measured, gets done.* Period.

Here's a real-world example related to driving:

At 55 mph, you travel about 80 feet per second. It takes about ¾ of a second for your brain to recognize a hazard, during which you travel 60 feet. Another ¾ of a second passes before your foot moves to the brake, traveling another 60 feet. Then your car takes 170 feet to stop. Altogether, you need roughly 300 feet of stopping distance behind another car. But who can practically measure 300 feet in real time?

Instead, drivers use the "3-second rule." Pick a stationary object; when the car in front passes it, count how many seconds before you reach it. If it's at least 3 seconds, you've got a safer following distance. This is an example of measuring what makes sense for your environment.

Yes, everything can be measured. I know that's bold but hear me out: everything in life is a process. Processes have a beginning, an endpoint, and inputs that affect the outcome. Waking up, taking out the trash, cooking, college, dating, marriage, raising children, loading the dishwasher, mowing the grass — all processes.

Since everything is a process, everything can be measured in some form or fashion. The challenge is figuring out *how*, *where*, and *when* to measure.

Now, a quick nerd moment — remember high school math?

$$Y = f(x)$$

Don't panic! This just means:

Outputs (Y) are the result of **interactions among inputs (x).**

Put simply, what happens in your life (*outputs*) comes from what you put in (*inputs*)—your habits, decisions, actions, mindsets, and attitudes. You may not control the outputs directly, but you have certain influence of the inputs.

People often want to measure the output (Y), but that's often too late to change things effectively — in my industry, we call those *lagging metrics*. When you only measure after the fact, it's hard to course-correct in time.

Have you ever gone canoeing? Imagine sitting in a canoe and trying to steer with an oar from the back. Like *lagging metrics*, it takes more time to turn the boat and less precise than taking the oar and paddling on either side of the canoe up front, like you would with *leading metrics*.

If you measure *only* the output (what's lagging) say, employee turnover — you're measuring the end-result, not the factors causing it.

Turnover rate = $f(x_1$ leadership, x_2 employee empowerment, x_3 competitive wages, x_4 organizational culture, x_5 employee satisfaction...)

By the time turnover is high, the damage is done — bad leadership, poor culture, low morale. Fixing that is costly and slow.

Instead, focus measurements closer to the *inputs* (what's leading) — leadership health, employee engagement, culture, salaries — so you can act early and have a better shot at preventing bad results.

Since spiritual maturity (Y) is hard to measure, focus on measuring the inputs: time spent reading the Word, prayer, fellowship, mentoring, kingdom-minded activities. No single input guarantees maturity, but together with the right heart, they position you for growth.

Having said that, don't throw out output (Y) measurements entirely — lagging metrics are still important to track overall progress. In business, leaders watch turnover, revenue, profits, and goals alongside the inputs — this is called a *balanced scorecard.*

In your spiritual journey, what does success look like? What indicators tell you, "Yes, I'm making progress!"? Maybe it's the consistent fruit of the Spirit, accountability from trusted partners, breaking free from emotional chains, or increasing spiritual activities.

Look back at your Actions and Initiatives from the previous section. How will you measure their effectiveness? If reading the Bible consistently is an action, define what "consistent" means and measure it. How many times per week? How often is the Spirit speaking to you through the Word? If your goal is to read the Bible in a year, how many books per month or week does that mean? The key is the document both *how much* and *by when/how often.*

This might seem tedious or obsessive, but I challenge that mindset. These daily actions build the foundation for your annual goals — the milestones on your Breakthrough journey. Precision and accountability in the small things lead to success or failure in the large things.

A quick but crucial warning: be careful not to fall into legalism. Measuring actions can easily slip into religious duty — doing things to check a box or earn spiritual brownie points. That's religion, not relationship. Religion is about rules and rituals; faith is about a heart posture. Jesus came to abolish the legalism of religion.

He has enabled us to be ministers of his new covenant. This is a covenant not of written laws, but of the Spirit. The old written covenant ends in death; but under the new covenant, the Spirit gives life. (2 Corinthians 3:6 NLT)

If your measurements lead to legalism, judgment, or spiritual suffocation, you've missed the point. But when your actions flow as worship from a pure heart, growth flourishes:

Blessed are the pure in heart, for they will see God. (Matthew 5:8 NIV)

One easy way to determine if you've shifted into legalism is if you start to feel condemnation or even self-hatred. On the other hand, the Spirit of God causes conviction. Condemnation and conviction may feel similar at first, but they come from very different places and lead to very different outcomes.

Condemnation, sourced from legalism says, "You messed up, so you're a failure. You're unworthy. You should hide." It's heavy, hopeless, and rooted in shame. Condemnation pushes you away from God and leaves you stuck, feeling disqualified. That's now how God speaks to His children – that's the voice of legalism, guilt, and the enemy (Satan.)

Conviction, on the other hand, says "This isn't who you are. Come closer – I have better for you." It's the gentle, guiding nudge of the Holy Spirit. Conviction leads to transformation, not despair. It invites you into healing, not hiding. It corrects, but always with love and hope.

See, legalism thrives on condemnation. It is performance based and says, "Do more, try harder, or else you don't measure up." But the Gospel of Jesus, the message of grace, brings conviction that restores our identity in Christ and reminds us all of this: *You are loved, even in your weakness. Now let's grow from here.*

My hope is you'll embrace the power of a pure heart, apply measurements wisely, keep yourself accountable, and pursue God with precision — so you will see Him more clearly.

Flip to page 112 and complete the rows labeled "Measurements" to keep building your personal Hoshin plan.

Accountability

Fact: I love a good cake. Having the right measurements in place to keep yourself accountable is only one layer in the cake. I mean, you want to have your cake and eat it too, right? Well, then you need more layers of accountability! We are all the sole owners of our own road trip, our goals, and milestones. However, there needs to be an honest and humble acknowledgment that we were not designed to travel alone.

> *Iron sharpens iron, and one man sharpens another. (Proverbs 27:17 ESV)*

> *Two are better than one, because they have a good reward for their toil. For if they fall, one will lift up his fellow. But woe to him who is alone when he falls and has not another to lift him up! Again, if two lie together, they keep warm, but how can one keep warm alone? And though a man might prevail against one who is alone, two will withstand him—a threefold cord is not quickly broken. (Ecclesiastes 4:9-12 ESV)*

Many people shy away from accountability. Recent and current events have helped to mold a society where deep interpersonal relationships are increasingly difficult—thanks to rapidly evolving technology, cultural shifts, social media, or a worldwide pandemic that made people feel safest through isolation. Regardless of the reason, this doesn't diminish the importance of having accountability through relationships. Some of you may find connecting closely with others difficult because of past trauma.

In warfare, creating separation in your opponent is a huge advantage. Getting members of your opponent isolated or alone is a sure-fire path to victory. Our enemy, Satan, strives to isolate us, making us easier to pick off.

Naturally, some of us tend to shy away from connecting with others, especially those with different backgrounds, life experiences, or personalities. But God did not intend for us to live isolated.

> *[For my hope is] that their hearts may be encouraged as they are knit together in [unselfish] love, so that they may have all the riches that come from the full assurance of understanding [the joy of salvation], resulting in a true [and more intimate] knowledge of the mystery of God, that is, Christ. (Colossians 2:2 AMP)*

In the corporate environment, whenever I launch a program, project, or initiative, I identify key individuals who ensure progress and completion. These key players always fall into one of four categories: Responsible, Accountable, Consulted, Informed.

Those I designate as *Responsible* are the true owners; the buck stops with them. This is their baby, their project, and they own it. The *Accountable* individuals have skin in the game—a vested interest in the outcome—and a strong enough relationship with the Responsible party to pry for updates or request status checks.

They could be business partners, peer team members, subordinates, or superiors. Those who are *Consulted* need to know what's happening or might be impacted by decisions. Those who are *Informed* simply receive notifications as an FYI. No project or initiative can succeed without this hierarchy of stakeholders identified and fully leveraged.

In your personal spiritual journey, having all four layers may be too big a cake to build (again—yes, I love cake). However, as the owner of your spiritual growth, you need to proactively and intentionally build an essential layer of accountable individuals in your life. On this road trip, you need to ensure that your proverbial front seat is occupied with a copilot, or two, or more. These are people you grant access to your life to check on your progress, keep you on track, and ensure your efforts and motivation don't fade. These people are vital to your success.

If you're married, your primary and most important accountability partner is your spouse. Your spouse should be your number one supporter, your loudest fan, and a primary source of encouragement (after God, of course). If that's not currently the case, be encouraged—there are plenty of resources available to help foster this dynamic. The Bible says two shall become one flesh.

> *And the two are united into one. Since they are no longer two but one. Let no one split apart what God has joined together. (Mark 10:8-9 NLT)*

This means your success is your spouse's success. Your lack of success is theirs, too. By default, your spouse should have a vested interest in the outcome. Beyond marital obligation, your spouse should be your loudest cheerleader. So, use that to your advantage—open lines of communication, be vulnerable, and allow them to hold you accountable.

Beyond your spouse, you'll need others as well. Selecting the right individuals isn't like picking teams at a playground kickball game. Picking favorites sometimes doesn't work out in your best interest. And picking only people you naturally click with can keep you trapped in your comfort zone. Just as we seek God's insight for Breakthrough objectives, finding the right accountability partners comes through seeking God's guidance and wisdom. He will send people your way in ways only He can.

For years now, I've been honored to be connected to four men I otherwise wouldn't have naturally chosen as accountability partners. Yet God, through answered prayer, placed them in my life to help bring greater growth and maturity. One lives tightly tucked inside his comfort bubble, one plans every minute of his day like clockwork and sees the world as black and white, one constantly asks questions I bet even Jesus would have a hard time answering, and one unapologetically lives life with his pedal to the metal. Then there's me, seemingly different than all of these.

They are all Godly men—but naturally, I would never have gravitated toward them. The beauty is that we not only click together, but we also thrive together. I'll be honest: my spiritual growth looked like a typical stock market graph for years—lots of ups and downs, high variation. Since becoming a team, my family can attest that my growth in spirit has been an exponential upward trend. Over time, God has continued to send men into my life—either to keep me accountable or for me to help hold others accountable.

God may have already placed someone in your life that you need to invite in as an accountability partner. Ask Him for wisdom as you identify these people and for Him to keep bringing the right ones to you. He is faithful and righteous to provide this need.

Vulnerability and access are keys—you give these individuals permission to check in, ask about progress, and even give you a loving kick in the pants if you get sidetracked.

For many, connecting with others is the hardest part. Do I ask them like it's a date? That's weird. Do I write an email explaining the goal and intent? How does that conversation even start? I won't promise it won't be awkward, but I will promise that if you only ever do what's comfortable, you'll never grow. Ever.

That said, it doesn't have to be weird or awkward—don't count on it being that way. People are more willing to connect than you think. It just takes someone (hint: you) to put pride aside and take the first step. So no, this isn't like asking someone out, nor do you need a thesis to explain everything. God will orchestrate intersections between you and others—you just must capitalize on them.

Was it awkward when Jesus appointed his disciples? I doubt it. They were in the right place at the right time—obviously orchestrated by God—and despite their differences, found an organic connection so strong they dropped everything and followed Him. In a similar way, as you interact with others, you'll sense a tug in your spirit. As you get to know them, you'll feel the natural desire to open up. The key is getting started. The key is spending time with people. Don't worry—we're not done with accountability yet; we'll dive into more aspects later in the book.

For now, flip to page 112 and complete the rows labeled "Accountability" to continue building your Hoshin plan; be sure to write down specific names of individuals.

CHAPTER 4

VEHICLE & EQUIPMENT

Now that you have a clear idea of the direction you're headed, some short-term milestones identified, key indicators on your dashboard set, specific actions outlined to get you there, and copilots chosen for the journey, it's time to make sure your vehicle is ready to roll. Having a reliable vehicle to transport you from here to there is, of course, a no-brainer — it's an absolute necessity.

In your life, this vehicle is the structure you've built or enabled, which ultimately propels you down the road toward your destination. Your 'vehicle' is a blend of your faith, behaviors, and activities — either running smoothly like a well-oiled machine or sputtering along, clunky and unreliable, leaving you stranded and searching for a lifeline.

What do beliefs, behaviors, and activities have to do with your ability to grow? Everything. The Bible tells us that man was created with three parts — spirit, soul, and body.

> *May God himself, the God of peace, sanctify you*
> *through and through. May your whole spirit, soul*
> *and body be kept blameless at the coming of our*
> *Lord Jesus Christ. (1 Thessalonians 5:23 NIV)*

Each part was uniquely created by God to fulfill a specific purpose. Beliefs are rooted in the deepest part of a person — their spirit. Behaviors come from the soul, the sum of thoughts, emotions, and decisions. Activities are the outward expression of beliefs and behaviors exhibited through the body. We'll explore each in detail.

Beliefs = Spirit

Every organization should have a value system — a set of underlying principles that guide how they bring products and services to market, how leaders lead, and how people respond to situations. Essentially, every organization has a corporate identity.

There are only two types of organizations: those intentional about their identity and those with an accidental identity. An organization with an intentional identity has completed the hard work of establishing non-negotiable core tenets. Leaders know why they're there and fully embrace the mission. Employees understand what they're stepping into and willingly assimilate to the culture if they want to be part of the team. When a strong culture exists, it shapes the behavior of everyone joining the team.

If a company hasn't been intentional about its identity, it ends up passively allowing the behaviors of whoever walks in the door to define it. This 'accidental' identity tends to be weak, inconsistent, and eventually fosters a toxic cycle that breeds poor behaviors.

People operate the same way. Did you know you have a spirit designed to connect with God through the Holy Spirit?

The Spirit himself testifies with our spirit that we are God's children. (Romans 8:16 NIV)

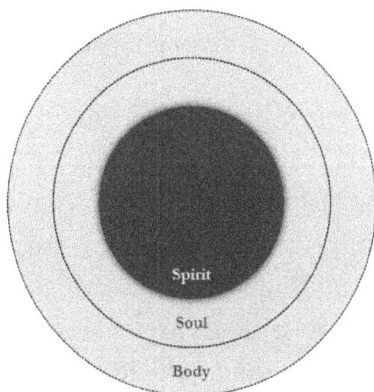

The purest, most authentic version of who you are exists in your spirit. This is your heavenly identity — uniquely created with purpose to fulfill a specific destiny. When you intentionally tap into this identity, it flows out from your spirit into your soul (behaviors) and ultimately shapes your actions (body).

But if your focus shifts away from who you were created to be and towards external influences, the opposite happens. Your actions begin to mirror the culture around you, your behaviors start to reflect the world's distractions, and your God-given identity gets choked out.

And the one on whom seed was sown among thorns, this is the one who hears the word, but the worries and distractions of the world and the deceitfulness [the superficial pleasures and delight] of riches choke the word, and it yields no fruit. (Matthew 13:22 AMP)

This applies whether you're single, married, or part of a household. If you have a spouse or children, establishing a Godly identity is even more critical — because your identity impacts not only your own life, but those you love.

For organizations, tough times come and go — just like in life. Storms, turmoil, and hardship are inevitable. But the one thing that withstands the test of uncertainty is a strong organizational identity. Technology, business strategies, processes, and people change — but identity should remain firm, unshaken by outside forces. In life's storms, your personal identity is the steel-reinforced crossbeam in your vehicle's chassis that keeps you safe on your journey.

I believe fully embracing your Godly identity is the key to living a life of growth in God's kingdom. Wondering why your prayers seem unanswered? Feeling like God isn't listening? Or like life is just a reaction to everything around you? The root cause always traces back to a lack of awareness of your identity.

Imagine my daughter — my own flesh and blood — waking up every morning and forgetting she's part of my household. She would forage for food outside or beg for help. But the truth is, she knows she's my daughter; she freely opens the pantry and helps herself to whatever she wants (especially lots of pickles). That's identity.

Similarly, are you fully convinced your identity is as a son or daughter of the King? If you are, you recognize everything has already been done on your behalf — the table is set, and all you have to do is reach out and receive.

> *He brought me to the banqueting house, and his banner over me was love. (Song of Solomon 2:4 ESV)*

There are over 7,000 promises in the Bible reserved for those God loves and calls redeemed — and if that's you, every one of those promises applies to you (yes, that includes you).

Behaviors = Soul

Most people think of behavior as a set of outward actions. This isn't wrong; however, psychologists agree that behavioral science begins with understanding the cognitive composition of a person. If you have recently interviewed for a job, you may have noticed that the questions asked are no longer black and white, aiming solely to screen for required skills. Employers are increasingly using Cognitive Behavioral Interviewing (CBI) to determine if potential candidates are a good fit for their organization and corporate culture. They are interested in your thought processes, your emotional intelligence, and your decision-making abilities.

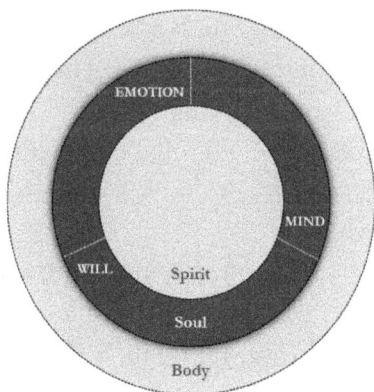

Guess what? God too is interested in your thought processes (*mind*), sentiments (*emotion*), and your abilities to make sound decisions (*will*). After all, He designed your soul with these innate abilities to help you succeed.

MIND

The mind may be the most important segment of your soul. The mind is the one function that directs so much of your life. In fact, I liken the mind to the steering wheel of your car. The direction of your mind will dictate where you end up. To keep it simple, what are you expending your mental energy on? What are you thinking about? How you answer this may be the very root of why you're not seeing the results in your life that you (and God) desire.

> *For those who live according to the flesh set their minds on the things of the flesh, but those who live according to the Spirit set their minds on the things of the Spirit. (Romans 8:5 ESV)*

What does it mean to set the mind on the Spirit? In the previous section, I explained that in your spirit, you will find the Holy Spirit constantly revealing things about your identity. As such, when you set your mind on the Spirit, you're focusing on who you are in God and coming into a fuller and deeper understanding of your true self – the self that God designed you to be.

It's no secret that I really enjoy motorsports, and I have owned and continue to own performance vehicles and motorcycles. I thoroughly enjoy tinkering, building, and working on cars and motorcycles. However, if I'm not careful with how much I think about car or motorcycle parts, I will find myself getting swept away with constant thoughts of motorsport projects. Once my mind starts thinking about parts, builds, and options, that hobbyist's love becomes a psychological stimulant, which snowballs into a sinking logic that maybe a few parts won't hurt the bank. Give it a few weeks, and you will see my checking account depleted of funds and a doorstep full of delivered car parts, awaiting countless hours of installation. What you set your mind on critically determines the physical outcome of many things in your life.

So practically speaking, how do you set your mind on the Spirit?

Sometimes, it doesn't seem like you can control what your mind does; it's like it has a mind of its own. Unfortunately, that's part of the fall of man; as man partook of the tree of knowledge, it introduced much good and much evil to the mind. However, the Bible talks about the ability to have your mind renewed so that you can experience more holy thinking through the washing of the water of the Word.

> *Don't copy the behavior and customs of this world, but let God transform you into a new person by changing the way you think. Then you will learn to know God's will for you, which is good and pleasing and perfect. (Romans 12:2 NLT)*
>
> *To be made new in the attitude of your minds. (Ephesians 4:23 NIV)*

That, my friends, is the key. Spending time in the Word of God is the key to mind renewal. As you allow the Word of God to infiltrate your mind, as you process the words and allow thoughts of His Word to settle, you begin to become more singularly focused on the things of God. Guess what happens then? Everything else becomes so much less important. To this day, I still have thoughts of car parts, and that's perfectly fine because I know that I'm spending infinitely more time thinking on the Word of God. If you win the war in the mind, the rest is downhill.

One critical thing to know is that the Bible isn't just a compilation of inspirational texts. The Bible is alive!

> *For the word of God is alive and active. Sharper than any double-edged sword, it penetrates even to dividing soul and spirit, joints and marrow; it judges the thoughts and attitudes of the heart. (Hebrews 4:12 NIV)*

> *It is the Spirit who gives life; the flesh is no help at all. The words that I have spoken to you are spirit and life. (John 6:63 ESV)*

The Bible, the Word, is a person.

> *So the Word became human and made his home among us. He was full of unfailing love and faithfulness. And we have seen his glory, the glory of the Father's one and only Son (John 1:14 (NLT)*

So, like you, someone who lives at the intersection of the physical realm and the spiritual realm, the Word has the ability to cross from the physical realm (as text on a page) to impact the spiritual realm. That is the true power of the Bible. When you read the Bible, as your physical eyes capture the images of the words, or your ears hear the words (or both!), your mind starts to interpret and process the words. When you then apply the lens of your Godly identity to these words, they become truth. This truth is what will set you free and be the way your mind experiences renewal, little by little, day after day.

> *Then you will know the truth, and the truth will set you free. (John 8:32 (NIV)*

It's important to remember that Satan also knows the value of your mind. He knows that the mind is the linchpin behind how every single person acts. Let's rewind history a bit — when mankind stumbled in the Garden of Eden, it was the mind which was the target of Satan's strategy. He knew that if he could get man to think thoughts that differed from God's Word (mind), it would lead to feelings of pride (emotion), which would result in a decision to eat from the wrong tree (will). This is exactly what happened. As I look back on my life, every single "bad decision" I have made was the byproduct of where I aimed my mind. Ultimately, when it comes to the mind, the goal is to possess the mind of Christ.

> *For who has understood the mind of the Lord so as to instruct him? But we have the mind of Christ. (1 Corinthians 2:16 ESV)*

The only way to accomplish this is to intimately know the Word of God.

EMOTION

Feelings are important. I can't believe I'm admitting that! As a guy, sometimes I like to invalidate feelings, labeling them as null or useless in their contributions. My wife knows this quite well (*yikes!*). However, admittedly, emotions can be a gauge of the health of the situation around you as well as the health of your inner being. Just like your mindset should reflect the Christ within, your emotions should also reflect the eternal life inside of you. If your palette of emotions tends to include a lot of anger, sadness, toil, pain, or frustration, it's time to allow the Holy Spirit to do a work within.

Too often, the emotional cycle that many people fall into is an entrapment technique used by the enemy to trick minds into thinking things they shouldn't. Let's face it, we have all witnessed people with wild mood swings and massive emotional ranges that change very frequently. When emotions are left unchecked, they tend to grow into an attention-seeking diva who loves to decide when and where to go. Instead of being led by the Spirit and a mind set on Christ, you can end up living a life led by emotion. This kind of life lacks purpose, direction, and often leads to a mantra of 'do what feels good,' which yields physical addictions and a lack of self-control. The fact is, you cannot be a spiritual being while solely led by emotions; they work against each other in that regard. Emotions are God-given and aren't going away; they should reflect the Godly things taking place within, rather than be an independent source of guidance.

While on the road of spiritual growth, you need to stay within the yellow lines so you get where you are going and so you don't side-swipe and interfere with others on their journey. I have seen too many friendships and marriages deeply impacted because people live relying solely on their emotions. Emotional self-control is not a restriction of self; it's freedom to operate in a way that God intended for you. The truth behind that self-control is that it's not as much 'self' control as it is Holy Spirit control. The Bible is very clear on what the fruit of the Spirit are.

> *But the Holy Spirit produces this kind of fruit in our lives: love, joy, peace, patience, kindness, goodness, faithfulness, gentleness, and self-control. There is no law against these things. (Galatians 5:22-23 NLT)*

These are Godly emotions which help reassure that you are staying within your lane. Then when you start to deviate from the path and begin driving in the berm of deep sadness or seething anger, your built-in lane assist — the Holy Spirit — should be activated to help you stay between the yellows. Feeling impatient? News flash, something's off! Feeling full of rage? Warning, you're veering off course! Your emotions act as instantaneous alerts to something being wrong.

WILL

This is the part of the soul that most directly influences the body. What the will decides, the body does. However, keep in mind that the mind and emotions dictate what the will does. Think of the will like the gas pedal of a car. It is the mechanism that ultimately propels the vehicle forward, but it is not where the power comes from nor the determining factor on where the vehicle goes. There is an engine that generates the power and enables the drivetrain. That drivetrain converts static power into propellant force. There is then a steering wheel to determine which direction to go in. All the gas pedal does is execute what every other component has been generating all along. In other words, it's kind of like a 'launch' button.

Your will launches everything that you have already decided in your mind and what your emotions feel like doing. All your will is doing is saying 'OK' to the rest of your soul, which enables your body to follow suit. Too often, people try to troubleshoot bad outcomes by blaming a lack of willpower or poor decision-making. The truth is, addressing bad decisions at the time of decision-making is like stopping a moving train. Most of the time, it's an exercise in futility.

In the business world, organizations often hold leaders accountable for their decisions while spending little to no investment in the leader to help them make informed decisions. Do they have the right analytical capabilities to make the right call? Do they have the emotional intelligence to read the situation? Without these capabilities that help set the stage, provide context, and enable the leader to make an informed decision, he or she may end up flipping a coin and praying for good odds.

In the same way, God has not designed you to live a life where you're set up for failure. God designed decision-making to be easy and effectively successful for you — IF you do it His way. When your mind is set on the things of heaven, and your emotions are contributing and not detracting, decisions become a no-brainer. When the Holy Spirit tells you to do something or not to do something, you're able to hear loud and clear, and then decide to act accordingly in effortless obedience. Ultimately, your will is mimicking His will. Just like the Lord's prayer says, *"Your will be done, on earth as it is in heaven."*

When you align your whole being — your mind, emotion, and will — with God through your spirit, you are bringing God's Kingdom into the earth.

Actions = Body

The third part of man is the physical body. This is the part of your being that God designed for you to interact with the physical world. I have mentioned previously that most of your physical actions are the downstream implications of the activity level in your spirit and soul. According to the Bible, your body really is not your own.

> *Do you not know that your bodies are temples of the Holy Spirit, who is in you, whom you have received from God? You are not your own; you were bought at a price. Therefore honor God with your bodies. (1 Corinthians 6:19-20 NIV)*

Spirit

Soul

Body

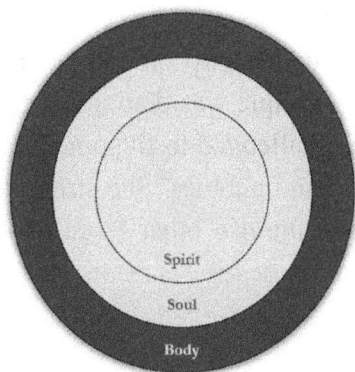

This means there is a level of discipline you can and should be applying to your day-to-day activities in order to glorify the One who you truly belong to. Unfortunately, much too often the most common obstacle (excuse) in forming any physical discipline is this: lack of time.

When trying to help leaders in the business world engage in critical leadership behaviors, the most frequently used excuse I hear is, *"I don't have time."* Time, like money, should be spent with priorities in mind. As a healthy reminder, leaders are placed into leadership positions because of their ability to positively influence and develop others — not simply because of their business savviness or acumen. Too often, leaders operate with an inverted priority mindset; their day-to-day operational duties become most important. They allow their full attention to be leeched by business firefighting, managing escalations, urgent emails and phone calls, or problematic situations. Over time, this flurry of activity becomes their priority, leaving critical leadership activities like coaching and development to fall to the wayside.

Franklin Covey taught the simple principle of Big Rocks[5], which I believe has a profound impact on both the business world and personal life. The principle was demonstrated by bringing up a volunteer who was challenged to fit some large rocks into a jar already full of sand and pebbles. She struggled to fit even one large rock, let alone the 4-6 other large rocks waiting on the table.

When priorities are not defined, we often fill our schedules with tons of little tasks or items of little importance, and we have a hard time understanding why the more daunting agenda items never get done. This leaves us feeling unaccomplished and frustrated.

As Covey's demonstration continues, he asks, "If you could do this exercise over, what would you do differently to ensure that the rocks can fit in the jar?" The volunteer says that she would start by putting in the big rocks first. As you can imagine, she starts with the big rocks, gets them all in, and then pours the pebbles and sand in. After a few shakes to allow things to settle, both the big rocks and every single pebble and grain of sand now fit in the jar.

The lesson learned here is to start with the top priority activities in your life — schedule or account for those first. Then add everything else in. The next logical question to be asked is, *how do I determine what is priority?*

I'm so glad you asked. Here are some things to consider:

- What ongoing activities would help you achieve your one-year objectives?

- What things should you be doing regularly that would help keep your mind, emotion, and will in a healthy state?

- What ongoing activities would strengthen you in your Spirit?

- What activities should you be dedicating regular time to for the sake of your spouse, children, or loved ones?

- What kind of mechanisms cause you to strengthening the level of accountability in your life?

Answer all of these, and you will have a pretty good idea of the Big Rocks in your life, which will help you weed out everything else that doesn't need to take place.

You may be asking, *what about activities related to work, chores, hobbies, church?* Listen, the Big Rocks that you identify using the questions listed above will help determine the activities that truly lead to life or death (spiritually and possibly even physically). Work, chores, hobbies, and even church are all good, but secondary. In fact, your ability to contribute effectively to these areas is completely dependent on your ability to be healthy in these Big Rock activities.

So, go ahead… prioritize the Big Rocks in your life. Go to page 113 and write down the Big Rocks in your life.

Big Rocks may change over time depending on the season that God has placed you in. The key to remember with any of these tools is not to carry a legalistic mindset. This shouldn't lead you to a list of must-dos and feelings to fulfill obligations. It's intended to promote the self-regulation of Godly habits in your life; it's a structured approach to keep you locked on the path that you're supposed to take. As your journey shifts, so will the parameters of the structure, and that's okay!

CHAPTER 5

FUEL

No matter how well-packed your bags are, how perfect your route is, or how ready your vehicle appears to be before the road ahead—if your car has no fuel, you're not going very far at all. The same is true for this journey of spiritual growth.

The center of your spiritual growth must be intimacy with God. It MUST be. He did not invite you into a religion of rituals or a mere checklist of moral behaviors. He does not require you to ascertain a level of holiness before He can interact with you. God invited you into a relationship built on proximity. Just like a car needs regular refueling to keep running, your being (as defined as tripartite, aka three-parts, in the last chapter) needs consistent time with God to keep growing.

The more you lean into His presence, the more you start to run on His strength, His grace, and His perseverance. That intimacy is what changes you from the inside out. It doesn't just move you forward—it transforms how you travel.

Did you know that the type of fuel you add to your car can affect its performance over time? In America, the three main types of gasoline at most gas stations are regular, mid-grade, and premium. Regular gas, typically 87 octane, is suitable for most vehicles. Mid-grade, often 89 or 90 octane, and premium, typically 91 to 94 octane, are designed for high-performance engines or vehicles with higher compression ratios. Using the wrong type of gas can lead to engine knocking, reduced performance, and potential long-term damage, especially if a car designed for premium fuel is given regular gas. It can also have a large impact on a car's gas economy, due to the engine running more or less efficiently based on the octane it was designed for.

Aside from the grades (octane levels) of gasoline, different gas stations also sell different tiers of gas. My wife rolls her eyes when it comes to this, but I personally only like buying gas as 2 or 3 gas stations because of the tier of gas they sell. I prefer buying Top Tier gas, even if it's a few more cents per gallon. Top Tier gasoline refers to a specific fuel standard developed by major automakers to ensure a higher level of detergent additives compared to the minimum required by the EPA. These additives help keep engines cleaner, potentially improving fuel economy, reducing emissions, and preventing performance issues like hesitation or stalling. Buying gas is much more complex now isn't it?

Spiritually, the same principle applies. We often end up filling our tanks with fuel that seems cheaper—fuel that costs less in terms of effort, convenience, time, or reputation. But the truth is, that kind of fuel is lower in quality and may damage us over time.

This "fuel" might come in the form of hobbies, relationships, dependencies, distractions—even things that seem good, like busyness or ministry. You can be doing things for God and still be running on low-octane fuel. Nothing substitutes for the real thing—God Himself.

God isn't impressed by our ability to perform. He's drawn to our desire to be with Him. Too often, Christians equate spiritual growth with spiritual activity. But proximity beats performance every time. The fuel for your journey ahead isn't found in doing more for God. It's found in being with Him. When you prioritize His presence, you'll find yourself running smoother, burning out less, and staying steady even when obstacles come your way.

You can have the perfect plan—complete with a Hoshin strategy and all the right milestones—but without God's presence, you'll eventually stall. Your engine won't respond. You'll be stuck when you least expect it. His presence isn't a luxury accessory for this journey—it's the fuel that makes the whole trip possible.

Let's talk about three essential spiritual fuels—prayer, the Bible, and worship. These aren't novel ideas by any means, but they certainly are non-negotiable.

Prayer

Prayer is vast, personal, and sometimes misunderstood. Thousands of books attempt to define it, categorize it, or teach formulas for doing it "right." But at its core, prayer is like a direct line to a spiritual gas station. It's not just about calling for help when the tank's low—it's about staying connected to the One who fills it.

Prayer is a direct connection to His presence. Prayer doesn't have to be polished or poetic. It just has to be honest. Sometimes it's words, sometimes silence. Sometimes it's a cry, a whisper, or simply, "God, I need You." Prayer is not begging. It's not persuading God or unlocking divine secrets with the right phrases or combination of words. It's a conversation—one that includes speaking, listening, vulnerability, and presence.

Rejoice always, pray continually. (1 Thessalonians 5:16-17 NIV)

The Greek word used for 'pray' here is (proseúxomai "pros-yoo'-khom-ahee" which literally means to interact with the Lord by swapping ideas. That's fellowship. Paris Reidhead once said, "Most Christians do not have fellowship with God; they have fellowship with each other about God."

Whether you're new to prayer or have been praying your whole life, it can sometimes feel overwhelming figuring out where to begin. Maybe the idea of praying has you panicked. Maybe you're just unsure of where to start. That's okay – you just have to decide to start somewhere!

Praying is our opportunity to get to know the God who created us, sustains us, and loves us. And yet, when we come before God, we often present Him with a list of things we want—like a grocery list. Can you imagine if you did that to your spouse or best friend? What a let-down! It wouldn't feel very much like a conversation.

When we talk to the people we care about in our life, we usually talk quite naturally, jumping from one topic to another, or we spend hours spilling out guts out over the details of our favorite topic, reveling in the feeling of being understood and loved.

That's the kind of connection we can have with God. Sure, we can absolutely come to Him when we need something. But we don't *only* pray then. Prayer is an ongoing conversation with God. A conversation that may not always change your circumstances, but that always changes you.

When we connect with our Creator, we are re-aligning ourselves to our very source—and that fuels us up. So unlike a gas station, you never want to detach from the pump; you never want the conversation to end.

The Bible

Reading the Bible is more than gathering information, understanding historical context, or even tracing a sequence of events. Many Christians treat the Bible like an ancient artifact—something to be *respected but rarely opened*. Others read it occasionally but never engage with it deeply.

But Scripture is not just another book; it is the living and active Word of God. It's actually all about revelation. Scripture is the living, breathing voice of God. It anchors you in truth, sharpens your discernment, and light up the road ahead.

> *But Jesus told him, "No! The scriptures say, 'People do not live by bread alone, but by every word that comes from the mouth of God.' (Matthew 4:4 NLT)*
>
> *Your word is a lamp to guide my feet and a light for my path (Psalm 119:105 NLT)*

When you soak in Scripture, which is actually a facet of the very person of God, it fills our minds with truth and our hearts with confidence in who He is. It's not just instruction—it's spiritual fuel for your being.

Having been in ministry for decades, I have seen the difference between people who truly engage with the Bible and those who don't. The difference is spiritual vitality. Those who immerse themselves in God's Word experience growth, clarity, and strength in their faith. Those who neglect it? They struggle, stagnate, and are easily swayed by the culture around them, kind of like a car running out of gas. They end up depleted from battling doubt, fear, and uncertainty. But the Bible is the fuel that strengthens faith.

The Word of God is the seed that brings spiritual rebirth. Just like God spoke before during the process of creation, in the Scripture He speaks to you as his new creation.

> *For you have been born again, but not to a life that will quickly end. Your new life will last forever because it comes from the eternal, living word of God (1 Peter 1:23 NLT)*

Without God's Word, we all would remain spiritually dead and stranded—just like the dry bones in Ezekiel's vision. But when we engage with Scripture, it breathes new life into our souls.

> *Then he said to me, "Prophesy to these bones and say to them, 'Dry bones, hear the word of the Lord! This is what the Sovereign Lord says to these bones: I will make breath enter you, and you will come to life. I will attach tendons to you and make flesh come upon you and cover you with skin; I will put breath in you, and you will come to life. Then you will know that I am the Lord.'" (Ezekiel 37:4-6 NIV)*

Have you ever felt like a sermon, teaching, or a passage of Scripture was reading you rather than you reading it? That's because the Bible is not just a book—it is a mirror that reveals who you really are.

> *For the word of God is alive and active. Sharper than any double-edged sword, it penetrates even to dividing soul and spirit, joints and marrow; it judges the thoughts and attitudes of the heart (Hebrews 4:12 NIV)*

When you read the Bible, you're not just informing your minds—you're exposing your heart. The Word of God convicts.

It challenges. It shows you where you need to change, where you need to grow, and where you need to go.

Faith isn't something we conjure up on our own or manufacture —it comes from hearing, reading, and absorbing the truth found only in God's Word. That's why the enemy works so hard to keep you distracted. Satan doesn't need to convince you that the Bible isn't true. He just needs to keep you too busy or entertained to engage with it.

As we traverse through a world of confusion, noise, and endless opinions, where do you turn for truth? The Bible is not just a spiritual book—it's the source of wisdom for everyday life.

What ultimately fuels you, makes you.

Worship

Whatever holds your attention will eventually have your devotion. If this very thing has your devotion, then it will certainly have your adoration. Worship is this very response of adoration, honor, reverence, and ultimately obedience. The life of worship is submitting to fellowship with God, over and over and over again.

Despite what you think, worship is more than music—it's a heart posture. It's the moment you say, "God, You are worthy," and everything else takes its rightful place. When you worship, you take your eyes off the road's distractions and place them back on the destination. It restores perspective. It recenters focus. Worship lifts you above what you see immediately in front of you and reminds you of the One who sees the whole route.

Christians often seek to live going from one defining moment with God to another defining moment with God. You can attend a conference and gain revelation, then sit back in contentment, then maybe see a prayer get answered. You thank God but work yourself back to your regularly scheduled programming of life, and over the course of life, your Christian experience is a series of encounters with God.

You may be saying to me, "I don't see a problem with that." Maybe not yet you don't or on the surface that doesn't feel like there's anything lacking. But what if I told you that going from defining moment to defining moment with nothing in between, is kind of like being married to your spouse and only spending time with them on date nights, I think you'd think about this whole thing slightly differently.

No "good mornings" and "good nights."

No excited reports of the great deals they struck at Homegoods.

No loving eye rolls from listening to all the dad jokes.

What stimulates (or fuels) any relationship to grow and be strong? Constant awareness and presence. It's in the moments of constant awareness and presence that you actually get to know God, and know His voice.

> *"I am the vine; you are the branches. If you remain in me and I in you, you will bear much fruit; apart from me you can do nothing (John 15:5 NIV)*

As one attached to the vine, you have the constant and uninterrupted ability to be linked to your source. You are attached! The moment you feel like you're breaking off from the source, worship and awareness brings you right back.

Unfortunately, there's not a singular set of tasks that I can give you that explicitly defines what living a life of worship looks like. If I did, I'd be giving you religious checklists to work through. But what I can offer you is one singular categorical way to consider what a life of worship looks like.

Therefore, I urge you, brothers and sisters, in view of God's mercy, to offer your bodies as a living sacrifice, holy and pleasing to God—this is your true and proper worship. Do not conform to the pattern of this world, but be transformed by the renewing of your mind. Then you will be able to test and approve what God's will is—his good, pleasing and perfect will (Romans 12:1-2 NIV)

A life of worship means that you subject (or submit) your entire being to this mission. Let every act of your body in living your life be an act of worship. In other words, let every act of your living body be a demonstration that God is your treasure, more precious than anything else.

When you live a life of worship, you are ultimately living with a higher degree of consciousness to God. This very awareness keeps you fueled for the mission ahead.

Every car on the road will eventually run out of fuel. Most cars have a warning light to let you know the gas is running low. I know many people who ignore this light and live life with lots of unnecessary suspense. I have only run out of gas once. It was late at night, I was young, on my way home and my fuel-level indicator was so low that it was way below the last line on the dashboard. This was before cars told you how more miles you had (which by the way, isn't always even accurate). Lo and behold, my car puttered to a stop as I coasted onto the berm on the highway.

If it wasn't for a kind and sweet middle-aged woman who stopped for a 19-year-old kid, walking and sulking down the offramp of a highway, it would have been a much longer night. She offered me a ride to the nearest gas station and even drove me back to my car! You better believe that I never made that mistake again.

Spiritually, we have indicators that let us know when we may need to refuel. We forget that we have constant access to a source of fuel and we often ignore the indicators, pushing ourselves to keep going even though we're running on fumes. I guarantee that you already can tell when you're running low on fuel.

You start snapping at people more than usual. Little things that wouldn't normally bother you suddenly feel overwhelming.

You're emotionally drained—and that's often a sign that you've been running in your own strength instead of God's.

Worship feels flat. Prayer feels dry.

You read the Bible but it doesn't land.

It's not that God is distant, but rather it's your tank running low. When we drift from God's presence, even holy things start to feel hollow.

When you're full of God's presence, fear doesn't have as much room to operate. But when that fuel runs low, anxiety creeps in and begins to dictate your decisions, priorities, and thoughts.

You stop caring. Not because you're mean, but because you're depleted. Your capacity to love others shrinks when you haven't been in close proximity to the One who is love. You start protecting yourself instead of pouring out.

You feel stuck, confused, and even unsure. That's often a signal that you haven't sat with the One who charts the course. God's presence doesn't always give you the whole roadmap, but it always gives you your next mile marker.

All this indicates that it's time to refuel.

The good news is that you don't have to drive miles to find a fill-up. When you focus on prayer and worship, God is always near. He's not hiding. He's not waiting for you to get it together. He's just waiting for you to pull over and be with Him again.

If you're serious about going the distance, you can't afford to coast. In order to push that gas pedal down, you need gas. You need it daily, you need it throughout the day. That's doesn't automatically mean some magical quantity of hours in a day, but it does mean intentionality. Maybe it's ten minutes of quiet prayer while you sip coffee. Maybe it's worship in the car while you commute, or a 15 minute walk after lunch while talking to Jesus.

The point is presence. Make space for Him and He will fill it.

> *You make known to me the path of life; you will fill me with joy in your presence, with eternal pleasures at your right hand (Psalm 16:11 NIV)*

All in all, the road trip you're on isn't about speed. It's about sustainability. If you want to go far, go fueled. Prayer, the Bible, and worship aren't just pit stops. They are the ever-available fuel stations that keep your spirit sensitive, your soul responsive to the right things, and your direction clear for the mission ahead.

CHAPTER 6

DASHBOARD & PASSENGERS

Imagine you are driving a car with no dashboard. Scary thought, isn't it? I mean, you have no idea how fast you're going. In fact, your only indicator of speed would be the relative pace of those around you. To some, this might actually be something you wish was reality; someone once said that "ignorance is bliss and so are triple-digit speeds." OK, I was the one who said this, and yes, I just quoted myself.

Without a dashboard, you certainly would not know how far you have traveled. You would have no idea when you would need to find a Buc-ee's to get more gas (and snacks). You would never know whether your car has issues until it's much too late. Even more, if the condition of the car at the onset was poor, I certainly would not recommend taking said car on a road trip, much less down the road to the grocery store. I think anyone with some common sense would agree to this.

So why do we allow ourselves to move forward in life without having dashboard elements present to show us all the necessary pieces of information to be successful? Dashboard elements? I'm sure you're wondering what that even means. In earlier chapters, we covered critical measurements to keep an eye on, to monitor progress in your growth. Well, that is only the starting point of living a dashboard life.

What is a dashboard life? A dashboard life simply means a visual life. Huh? What does that mean, you ask? It simply means that you are able to intentionally create some in-your-face reality checks when you have visual representation of the things that matter most. Let me expound.

In the business world, when the subject of performance and metrics arises, many leaders create an environment of employee anonymity in hopes of not creating an atmosphere of peer-to-peer judgment or making someone feel called out. What business leaders don't realize is that in doing so — albeit with good intentions — they are in fact breeding a culture that lacks the ability to drive accountability.

The most successful workforce is one that holds open accountability to specific, measurable, achievable, relevant, and time-bound objectives, including those who are 'in charge.' One of the critical contributors to success is clear visibility to individual and collective progress toward these objectives.

When our kids were younger, my wife and I started holding weekly family meetings (huddles) that covered a variety of topics. These meetings weren't terribly long, but lengthy enough to cover things like everyone's general mood, recognition & thanksgiving for one another, events & activities, and even the menu for family meals. Everyone was also accountable to do a recap of what their goals were for the past week, which led to the most valuable discussion: issues.

See, unless we were able to first openly identify a pattern of missing goals, we were never forced to think (and talk) about the issues that prevented the goals from being achieved. If we were to experience success, then we would need to focus on overcoming those issues and obstacles.

In similar fashion, businesses run into hundreds of issues daily, but most of the time they stay hidden in the depths of processes and great employees. In my world of business consulting, we call this the hidden factory — when there are parts of the process that diminish the quality or efficiency of the desired outcome, all while consuming valuable resources. For many companies, they have some incredible people who are kings and queens of "workarounds" that mitigate the issues but never solve it.

Imagine that you were on the Titanic on April 14, 1912, but what if ONE condition was different? The same time of night, same temperature, same route, and same ship. What if the difference was the height of the water level? At 11:35 p.m. that night, lookouts on the ship first spotted the iceberg a quarter mile ahead. Five minutes later, the ship sideswipes the iceberg. What if the ship was traveling in water that was just 20 feet less shallow?

It's been calculated that the lookouts would have spotted the iceberg 5½ miles away (instead of a ¼ mile) and would have had an additional six minutes to react and change course. If you were on the ship that night, I think you would agree that the mere 20 feet of extra visibility is a great thing. The only downside is that the story of Jack and Rose would be less dramatic. Maybe that is actually a good thing?

So, we can agree that lowering the water level is a good thing in order to see the things that cause us to slow down, redirect us, or even cause us to capsize.

If there is value in making problems and obstacles more visible, then there is value in making the work measurable and visible as well. With the right leadership mindset, this visibility allows for team discussions and problem-solving to take place aimed at solving the issue — versus aiming efforts at personal performance improvement plans for that individual.

In your journey of spiritual growth, this exact principle can be applied — create visibility to what you are measuring, so that week by week does not go by without attention being drawn to what needs improvement. If one of your goals includes daily time in the Word, nothing says 'hello, you're about to hit an iceberg' like seeing four red consecutive dots on a physical chart that indicate the four straight days you've missed scripture reading.

Without this physical reiteration of missed metrics, it's so much easier to mentally dismiss the behavior. Instead, visual representation of the misses has 43% more effectiveness in getting the habit back on track.

After three days of missing your reading, you would ideally call a timeout with your 'team' (you, yourself, and you), and dig a little deeper as to why you keep missing time in the Bible. Doing this may lead you to remember your decision to read the Bible right before bed — and now you realize that you keep going to bed too late. So you decide to work toward an earlier bedtime or perhaps try a different time of day to read. Either way, you are actively working to get PAST the obstacle, versus giving up and having no physical visual accountability to stare you in the face.

What gets seen gets done!

Human nature, theologically speaking, is always at odds with God's nature. Thanks to the sequence of events that took place in the Garden of Eden, the natural disposition every person seemingly defaults to in this physical world is not the same disposition that God originally intended for us, His beautiful creation. Buried within this fallen natural disposition is a propensity to let things go, be passive, subscribe to laziness, or wait until crisis to act.

I press on toward the goal for the prize of the upward call of God in Christ Jesus. (Philippians 3:14 ESV)

In contrast, a Godly nature is represented by proactivity, wisdom, and intentionality. This intentionality is arguably difficult to carry out if there is no visibility.

Specifically, I contend that it is nearly impossible to be intentional with the desired outcomes if you don't have visibility to where you've been, where you're at, and what direction you're going in. Let's dive into each of these three views.

Where You've Been

Everyone has passed key life milestones that they can reference as significant defining moments in their life. Whether it's major victories or dreadful defeats, our lives are ultimately a composition of many, many critical moments. When you have traversed with God by your side, there will be such a vast archive of defining moments where He has delivered you, provided for you, or proved His goodness to you.

Now we all know these characteristics of faithfulness are found throughout scripture. God certainly doesn't need you to be the reinventor of this message. However, as a Christian, as one who is born again through Christ and has received the inheritance, you are called to be representatives of who He is. That is, you are to re-present through your life how good He truly is. Whether it is to inspire others at a future date or to be a testimony to the friends He has placed in your life for the present time, when you make known God's eternal goodness and faithfulness in your life, it will produce a ripple effect through this natural realm that you occupy.

What does all this mean in a practical sense to have a dashboard indicator for where you've been? Try this. Try hanging up the very scripture that you relied so heavily on when God brought you through something difficult, like depression. Or how about finding a frame to put the medical bracelet that said you had cancer — which God healed you of. Or find that picture of the crummy apartment that you used to live in, you know, before you found God's provisional promises to be true, and hang it somewhere in your nicer, roomier homestead.

It doesn't even need to be references to such miraculous events. Put a piece of paper in your wallet with the date you decided to follow Jesus. The point is to make it visible and located somewhere you see it often.

God is faithful in the big things as He is in the little daily mundane things. The point being these mementos act as reminders for yourself in times where you may find yourself lacking spiritual strength. These mementos act as visual cues to bring your mindset back to that place of thanksgiving. As you enter into His gate with thanksgiving, you find yourself falling back in line with a life of faith.

In Joshua 4, God instructs Joshua to have the Israelites build a monument to commemorate the miraculous crossing of the Jordan River. Specifically, they are to take twelve stones (*there's that numeric specificity again*) from the riverbed, where the priests stood, and set them up at their camp. The intent of this instruction was so later in life, when the monument was seen, it would serve as a memory cue for generations.

So that all the peoples of the earth may know [without any doubt] and acknowledge that the hand of the Lord is mighty and extraordinarily powerful, so that you will fear the Lord your God [and obey and worship Him with profound awe and reverence] forever. (Joshua 4:24 AMP)

These personal symbols also are great testimonies for believers and non-believers alike, painting a picture of who God is in your life and what He is capable of in their lives. God talks about signs, wonders, and miracles as effective tools to stir up the right kind of curiosity in people who don't believe. Sometimes, people don't believe stories of God's goodness until they hear that the main character is someone they know. All of a sudden, it goes from a tall tale of fictional religion to a true encounter with God. Little do you realize that your story is the miracle that someone else is waiting to hear in order to believe in God.

Where You Are

We all go through seasons of life where our needs vary and what propels us forward changes. When something motivates you, you need to take full advantage of that by putting it front and center in your life. This is essentially a harnessing effort to capitalize on momentum.

In many churches, there is encouragement to seek God at the beginning of the year for a word or thought to carry through the year—yup, a Word of the Year. If this sounds familiar and God has given you a seasonal motivator, such as a word or phrase, then plaster that everywhere! Make it visible!

When He gives you a word of knowledge or sends verses your way, write them out, print them, and "decorate" your house with these reminders. If you currently find yourself in a struggle, find scriptural anchors that bring you peace amidst the struggle and make them visible wherever you go.

Besides the psychological reminder, when you add the habit of reading these verses aloud when you see them, you unlock the spiritual principle of building faith. Faith comes by hearing, right? What happens when you hear yourself speak truth over and over again? Exactly.

In college, I lived in an old, converted fraternity house with a bunch of guys. It was old, dumpy, gritty—the perfect setup for thrifty (aka poor) college guys. Occasionally, we would hear wildlife in the attic—squirrels, to be exact—and had the distinct pleasure of listening to them play tag in the attic and between the walls at 6 a.m. on a weekend.

I distinctly recall one roommate getting so fed up with the noise that he grabbed a CO_2-powered BB gun and started shooting into the ceilings and walls. The BBs went through the walls and ceilings, but I'm pretty sure he never came close to hitting any squirrels. The issue wasn't bad aim or inadequate tools—it was that he lacked visibility of the pests' current whereabouts.

One reason Visual Management works in the business world is that it makes current issues and problems visible. Here's the kicker: when you make issues and problems visible, it's not just visible to you but to everyone. Yikes!

With clients, we often use simple colors to indicate the health of the organization or what we're tracking. Green generally means good and on-target, yellow means at-risk, and red means behind or off-target. The health of an organization could be all red (bad), but what's the effectiveness and ability to course-correct if only a few key leaders know? What if the entire team could see red indicators showing something had gone awry?

Do you think it becomes just the leaders' problem to fix, or does it now become an all-hands-on-deck situation?

When you make current problems and issues visible, you enable and empower problem-solving at all levels. If problems aren't visible, chances are you're kicking the can down the road, and you'll continue to fall victim to the byproducts of the same issue repeatedly, eroding future success.

As an individual, you can make what matters to your current life visible. As a family, you too can make what matters to your current lives visible. Remember those weekly meetings I previously mentioned? Below is an example our family used to help align ourselves with what mattered. It also visually represented when our current results didn't match our intentions.

	Thanks!	Monday	Tuesday	Wednesday	Thursday	Friday	Saturday	Sunday
Announcements - Soccer cancelled this weekend - gate for Lilah **1**	**4** Titus							
Inspiration - Love is patient, love is kind, it does not envy, it does not boast, it is not proud. **2**	Sarah Ethan Zoey							**5**
Issues - Arguing - Putting stuff away/back **3** - Sharing - Lilah - Self-control	Events **6** Menu **7**	Zoey Piano GM Meatloaf	Etta Soccer Tacos	Tc/Sc meeting@ FLC 5:30 Chix Casserole	Zoey Soccer BLTs	Beef Stir-fry	Out	Tc out Watch Karmon TBD

Like I mentioned earlier, every week our family gathered for a brief meeting to review how the prior week went and how the current one is going.

We decided as a family that we wanted to be thankful, inspiring, planful, and respectful & loving toward each other. As such, we tracked elements and behaviors that would create this kind of environment.

Each of us, assigned a specific color, would give everyone else a colored dot under their name if we felt we received kindness and loving interactions from that individual. We did this for a week and started to see a pattern—that someone might have had a bad day that week. We provided instant support, words of affirmation, and encouragement.

We did this exercise for a month and began to notice that one of the kids was less loving to their sibling on a regular basis. We had just made an invisible (but palpable) issue visible! Once visible, it wasn't about blame—it became a problem-solving opportunity. It was a chance for us as a family—and for us as parents—to help our child become more kind to their sibling.

Openly discussing the visible misses became open dialogue that became teaching moments so that current behaviors could be adjusted to fit the culture we were trying to uphold. A visible problem is a fixable problem.

Where You Are Going

Remember the Breakthrough Goals you identified on page 111? Remember the 1-year goals you named? Make those visible! The more often you see them, the more you're reminded they exist.

Of course, there's always a risk of seeing something so often that it becomes normalized. That's why as part of your ongoing Annual goals (also identified on page 111), you need to have dedicated time to review these objectives.

In the business world, some organizations dedicate entire walls to create a mural of their Hoshin Strategy. This way, everyone in the organization knows what they are here for and how they will contribute.

It is healthy to regularly review your progress, pray over your goals, and allow the Spirit to adjust things as time goes on. This creates a cycle of progress → review → revision → repeat that ultimately becomes growth. You won't look back and see the same you. You won't look forward with futility, thinking it will never happen. When you make progress, everything is indeed possible.

What about dream or vision boards? Do some research on this— I dare you. It's yet another visual tool for you to aim your sights on. These things could be redundant with your breakthrough objectives—that's fine! They can also include other things you want or hope for.

The so-called magic of vision boards isn't that once you pin something on a board it magically appears. It's that when you pin something and see it every day, it becomes part of your thought process. It's the exact same principle as setting your mind on the Spirit.

Your life yields results based on what you set your mind and thoughts to. What better way to guide your mind than to use visual cues to accomplish this?

Passengers

Ah, no road trip is complete without the company of fine friends with whom you don't mind sharing music, conversation, and nutritious snacks from Buc-ee's.

In the chapter 3, we discussed accountability as a critical key to success. Just like in real life, a counterpart on a road trip can help you stay awake and ensure you're not veering where you shouldn't be. However, the benefits don't end there.

> *When we get together, I want to encourage you in your faith, but I also want to be encouraged by yours. (Romans 1:12 NLT)*

As the Bible teaches, we were never intended to live life alone. This is greater than just accountability to keep us on track. We need allow people around us in the roles of supporters, mentors, and mentees.

First and foremost, find yourself a local church or group of believers. Too many Christians think the Rambo-model of Christian-walk is realistic and sustainable. You cannot traverse the Christian growth process without being plugged into the Body. Sorry, it can't be done. A person is not a person unless connected to a body.

God's completeness cannot exist unless there's a body associated with it—like a bride and her groom, or a vine and its branches. Both are required to create life. The Bible doesn't say what "kind" of church you should be part of. It doesn't have to be a mega-church, a certain denomination, style of worship, or have specific attributes. Whether it's a massive congregation of 50,000 or a humble home group of five, the key is regular gathering with the saints—aka the sanctified ones.

The only criteria I advise is to be with people who love the Word of God and is where God has led you.

If you don't already have someone more senior in your life—a spiritual father or mother who has gone through more life seasons—pray for such a mentor. Having godly wisdom in your life is never a bad thing. The Bible says much about this:

> *The way of a fool is right in his own eyes, but a wise man listens to advice. (Proverbs 12:15 ESV)*

> *Where there is strife, there is pride, but wisdom is found in those who take advice. (Proverbs 13:10 NIV)*

> *Let the message about Christ, in all its richness, fill your lives. Teach and counsel each other with all the wisdom he gives. Sing psalms and hymns and spiritual songs to God with thankful hearts. (Colossians 3:16 NLT)*

Even some of God's most used individuals had mentors God placed in their lives: Moses to Joshua, Elijah to Elisha, Paul to Timothy, Jesus to His disciples, Eli to Samuel, Solomon to the Queen of Sheba, Daniel to Nebuchadnezzar, Naomi to Ruth. The list goes on.

On the flip side, there is tremendous benefit in having younger, less mature Christians in your life to care for. Every parent steps into this role by default, modeling Christ for their children. But there are others God places on your heart who can benefit from your influence.

People are watching your life now and will come with questions when they see your transformation. God created us to be vessels that overflow—to others—and not just containers. As conduits of love and grace, we are called to care for those younger or less mature, as that is the natural order in His Kingdom.

Go back to your Breakthrough goals, or even your Annual goals. I would guess most of them impact others. No course set by God is self-serving. No growth is for the sole sake of oneself. When it comes to spiritual growth, everything is ultimately for God and His grand purpose: to expand His Kingdom to others.

When you place people in your life you can impact, your spiritual growth impacts them. As you journey on, as the driver, you are responsible for your passengers. Your success is their success. Your growth results in their growth. Your pursuit of Christ causes them to pursue Him too.

> *In the same way, let your light shine before others, so they may see your good works and give glory to your Father who is in heaven. (Matthew 5:16 NIV)*

Go to page 113 and add the names of passengers that you believe are part of your road trip.

CHAPTER 7

ISSUES & PREVENTATIVE MAINTENANCE

So, you're cruising along on your road trip. Tunes are cranked, you're making good progress, ahead of schedule, you seemingly know where you're going, and you've got great company riding shotgun and your backseat. As you round a bend, out of nowhere, you see orange signs up ahead: road closed, detour, obstacle.

Suddenly, things are not so smooth. You ask yourself, *What happened?* You realize you turned your GPS off because you thought you knew the way. Were there signs you missed? Your passengers say yes—they tried to warn you, but your music was too loud to hear them. Now, you're struggling with a weak GPS signal, low on gas, no map handy, and no other cars in sight— you're in a remote spot. So, what do you do now?

It doesn't take a seasoned veteran to know not everything goes according to plan. The fact is, we're always engaged in a battle—not against flesh and blood, but in the spiritual realm.

> *For we do not wrestle against flesh and blood, but against the rulers, against the authorities, against the*

cosmic powers over this present darkness, against the spiritual forces of evil in the heavenly places. (Ephesians 6:12 ESV)

For though we walk in the flesh, we are not waging war according to the flesh. For the weapons of our warfare are not of the flesh but have divine power to destroy strongholds. We destroy arguments and every lofty opinion raised against the knowledge of God, and take every thought captive to obey Christ. (2 Corinthians 10:3-5 ESV)

There are always forces working hard to pull you away from the dominion you have as son or daughter of God. We live in this world, but it's ruled temporarily by Satan, the adversary. Because of this, distractions, plots, and schemes bombard us constantly, attempting to derail our journey.

Too often, I meet businesses and leaders who expend energy fighting the same battles over and over again. The battles might wear different masks, but the root issue remains the same. You cannot expect different results if you keep doing things the same way. Put simply: change your approach, and your results will change. This requires shifting your mindset from reaction to prevention. Benjamin Franklin once said, "An ounce of prevention is worth a pound of cure."

Enter *Poka-Yoke*[6] — pronounced *"PO-ka yo-KAY"*. No, it's not some fancy new sushi dish, but a Japanese term meaning *mistake-proofing* or *error prevention*. Yet another concept from the expansive Lean toolkit. Look around you: outlets on the wall have specific prongs to prevent incorrect connections. USB ports are designed so you can only insert them correctly (even if it takes a couple of tries). Microwaves won't run if the door is open. These design elements prevent mistakes that could cause malfunctions, harm, or worse.

I believe God is the ultimate originator of Poka-Yoke. Consider the human body: intricately designed with built-in fail-safes. Take the heart, for example. Your circulatory system delivers oxygen and nutrients, while removing waste. What if blood flowed backwards? Catastrophic. Thankfully, your heart's valves and ventricles are designed to allow unidirectional flow — a perfect Poka-Yoke mechanism.

As your Creator, God delights when you adopt a preventative mindset to minimize issues in your life. So, what can *you* poka-yoke in your life? What problems are preventable? What isn't? This isn't about having a crystal ball to predict the future. The Bible has no magic sphere for seeing what's ahead. Rather, it's about positioning yourself under God's authority and grace, staying alert to problems so you can address them early before they grow out of control.

When the Spirit of truth comes, he will guide you into all the truth, for he will not speak on his own authority, but whatever he hears he will speak, and he will declare to you the things that are to come. (John 16:13 NIV)

God, through the Holy Spirit, wants to guide you as you walk into the future. The word translated "tell" or "show" here comes from the Greek *odego*, meaning a guide who leads a traveler safely through unknown territory. The Holy Spirit knows the way you should go—how to avoid every trap and attack. When you step into unfamiliar territory, surrender control and let the Spirit lead you. He wants to show you the exact route to reach the place God has placed in your heart.

This ministry of guidance was evident even when Jesus was on earth. In John 11, Jesus was led by the Spirit not to go immediately to Bethany when Lazarus was sick. The hostile religious leaders were waiting to trap Him. Jesus waited two days—until Lazarus had died—before going. His obedience to the Spirit's timing allowed Him to avoid confrontation and perform a powerful miracle safely.

In Acts, the Holy Spirit warned the early church of a coming famine. Because believers responded to this prophetic word, they prepared and weathered the hardship well. The Spirit also prevented Paul and his team from going to Bithynia, leading them instead to Macedonia through a vision. Paul obeyed immediately, and great fruit followed.

Without the Holy Spirit's guidance, you're left to navigate on your own. That's a scary thought—wasted time, energy, money, and needless tears. Ain't nobody got time for that! The Holy Spirit sees what you cannot, knows what you don't, and understands the best, safest paths. He is a wise leader—let Him lead.

If you've resisted His guidance before, don't make that mistake again. Let Him take your hand, and He will safely guide you to where God wants you to go.

Interval Maintenance

Picture yourself lying awake the night before a long cross-country drive. Your mind races with all the to-dos, the last-minute packing, and snacks. Double-check your alarm. Can you even sleep, overwhelmed by excitement and nerves? Then it hits you: *When was the last oil change?* Battery health? Windshield fluid? Tire tread? Coolant levels? Has the car been serviced recently?

You wouldn't take a car that's been sitting idle for five years on a 1500-mile journey, right? Likewise, a life charging forward without regular "maintenance" carries risks. God is always ready and willing to ensure you're cared for—to give you tune-ups whenever needed. After all, you're on assignment; you're commissioned. He needs you in tip-top shape to fulfill your mission.

> *Though they stumble, they will never fall, for the LORD holds them by the hand. (Psalm 37:24 NLT)*

> *Do not fear [anything], for I am with you; Do not be afraid, for I am your God. I will strengthen you, be assured I will help you; I will certainly take hold of you with My righteous right hand [a hand of justice, of power, of victory, of salvation]. (Isaiah 41:10 AMP)*

> *Don't worry about anything; instead, pray about everything. Tell God what you need, and thank him for all he has done. Then you will experience God's peace, which exceeds anything we can understand. His peace will guard your hearts and minds as you live in Christ Jesus. (Philippians 4:6-7 NLT)*

So what does a tune-up with God look like? How do you live a life of preventative maintenance?

It starts with structure. Structure exposes excuses, laziness, and shortcomings. Planning reveals maturity. Systems force you to slow down, show up, and stop winging it. Hope alone is NOT a strategy. Hope without infrastructure breeds instability.

Ever tried finding a small object in a messy closet or cooking on a cluttered countertop? You probably couldn't find what you needed quickly, slowing you down and frustrating you. Even familiar tasks become harder in chaos.

> *For God is not a God of disorder but of peace (1 Corinthians 14:33a NIV)*

> *But everything should be done in a fitting and orderly way. (1 Corinthians 14:40 NIV)*

I now introduce to you the concept of 5S. The 5S Methodology[7] was created to solve exactly these issues in manufacturing—to help organizations stay agile and competitive. It boils down to the saying: *A place for everything, and everything in its place.* The 5S stand for five principles, each beginning with "S." Not rocket science, just simple, practical order.

You might know Marie Kondo and her "KonMari" method[8], which simplifies and declutters homes. Followers report better focus, clearer decision-making, and improved prioritization.

While decluttering and simplifying are part of 5S, it also teaches how to do these tasks efficiently and sustainably.

No process is effective unless it's sustainable.

Now, imagine applying this methodical approach to your relationship with God. Maybe your spiritual life is as cluttered and confusing as that messy countertop. Or maybe you have a good walk with God but want to make it better, more sustainable.

The 5S Methodology can provide the structure you need.

Seriri (Sort)

Sorting creates a more productive workspace by removing unneeded clutter (and eliminating distractions). It also is the first step toward opening up space for other uses. Think about this as sifting or sorting the things in your life. The goal is to identify and ultimately remove any distractions or obstacles that you think might cause you to sin, and/or be the god in your life.

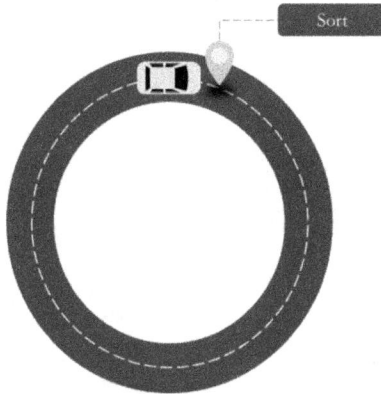

These distractions may take on the form of many different things. Bad things like drugs, alcohol, vices, sinful temptations. Or good things like friends, family, work, school, relationships, sports, etc. Remember, anything can have the propensity to cause you to love it more than love God.

You shall have no other gods before me. (Exodus 20:3 NIV)

God desires to have a deep relationship with Him. This means your love for anything else must never be greater than your love for God. By being proactive to identify and remove all these things to get your life on track is the beginning of this process.

Seiton (Straighten)

The Straighten step thoroughly organizes the items that remain after sorting, making frequently used items easily accessible and providing every item a clear and easy-to-find home. In a production environment, Straighten enables every item to have a specific home where it can be easily found and to which it can be easily returned. It reduces the waste from excess motion, as items are placed in more ergonomic locations. It is also the second step on the path to opening up space that can be used strategically toward the goal of improving production.

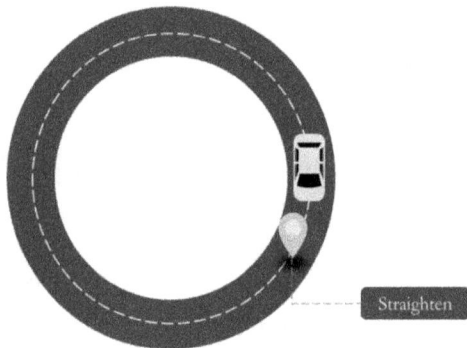

Straighten

Did you know that Jesus was a fan of this sort of organization? When 5,000 people were hungry in a remote area, Jesus took the lead in performing a miracle with five loaves of bread and two fish. The very first thing He instructed was a command of organization.

> *Then Jesus directed them to have all the people sit down in groups on the green grass. So they sat down in groups of hundreds and fifties. (Mark 6:39-40 NIV)*

Would the miracle have taken place had Jesus not straightened up the situation? I can't imagine this detail being here for no reason.

In your spiritual growth, after removing (SORTING) the distractions that occupy your idle time or steal your attention, take inventory of all the things that bring you closer to God. Things like reading the Bible, engaging in worship, fellowship with other believers, serving those in need, evangelizing, or praying. Straighten these things up in your life by making them more accessible.

In this instantaneous culture, we oftentimes are way better at making excuses why we can't engage in these healthy habits than actually doing them. The goal of Straightening our lives is to remove excuses and reduce wasted opportunities.

Everyone can have a Bible with over 100 versions on their phone nowadays. Keep worship playlists handy on Spotify or Apple Music. Always carry ten to twenty dollars in cash to help a random person in need. Carve time aside every week to ensure you're making time for other believers. Make all these things EASY to execute, EASY to participate in, and EASY to access.

Seisou (Shine)

In an operational environment, Shine helps create a work environment that engages and empowers operators by giving them more responsibility and agency over their work area. It also helps them identify problems before they interfere with production. The Shine step elevates the work area by ensuring thoroughly cleaned and inspected tools, equipment, and other items. It also can include routine maintenance on equipment.

Shine

For example, in a clean work environment, it is much easier to spot emerging issues such as fluid leaks, material spills, metal shavings from unexpected wear, hairline cracks in mechanisms, etc.

As a follower of Jesus, we are always looking to Him as the standard – remember, He's six sigma? He's the measuring stick for what is Holy, what is righteous, and what is love. For you to Shine means you focus on cleaning your heart on a constant basis by praying, thanking, and worshiping God regularly.

> *...Anyone who comes to Him must believe that He exists and that He rewards those who earnestly seek Him. (Hebrews 11:6 NIV)*

This pursuit of Jesus as the standard allows you to constantly be evaluating your life for emerging areas that don't match with what God intended for your life. This pursuit puts you in motion to seek Him daily, and God promises to reward His children who continue to talk to Him.

God calls us to pursue a life of holiness, which is a step above just being clean. A Godly life is a holy life – one that reflects and represents what is right. This doesn't mean perfect, this doesn't mean flawless, this doesn't mean a life without issues.

This just means that our identity is anchored in the One who is perfect, the One who is flawless, and the One who fixes issues. A holy life is a repentant life. A holy life is a forgiving life. A holy life is a humble life. A holy life is a submitted life.

Seketsu (Standardize)

The Standardize step is the bridge between the first three 5S steps (Sort, Straighten, Shine) and the last step (Sustain). In this step, your goal is to capture best practices which makes 5S repeatable. It transforms 5S from a one-off project to a reproducible set of activities.

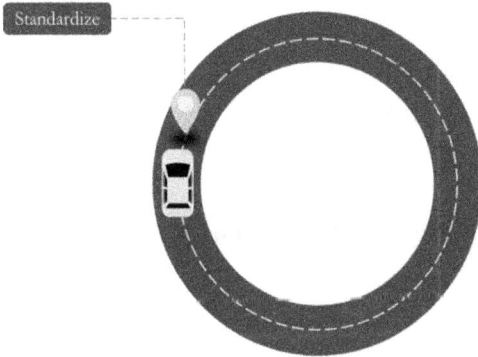

Have you ever attended a conference or an event where your heart, mind, and spirit are stirred up, and you leave all charged up, on fire, ready to take the world? You tell yourself you're ready to do all the things, talk to all the people, and change your whole life. I grew up going to youth conferences called Mountaintop, where for a week we would worship, compete in games, hear inspiring messages, and walk away ready to take territory. Fast forward two weeks from camp departure, and many of us found ourselves in a place of depression and boredom. The problem was never the height of these conferences. The Mountaintop Experience, as we called it, was not a sustainable expectation for daily life. As a young person, we never wanted that experience to end, and when it did, and we were back to normal and mundane things, life just felt as low as the deepest valley.

Life with God isn't always high, nor is it always low. The human experience is a beautiful composition of all elevations. The key is focusing on a sustainable pace. Whether climbing a steep mountain or descending into a pit, the pace of your spiritual life is important. Being regimented, being disciplined, and having ongoing standards is the key.

To experience this, you can go as far as creating a schedule that will put you on track with the activities that draw you closer to God. Add your worship schedule to your daily planner. Add time to pray. Add fellowship blocks. You make plans to see friends, plans to pay bills, plans to work – why would we not make plans to follow Jesus?

Keep your plan structured. For daily practices, you can include things like prayer, worship, and reading the Bible. For weekly practices, you can include things like church gatherings, life groups, Bible study, community outreach, and family prayer.

For monthly practices, you can include a corporate prayer night and fasting.

For yearly practices, you can include things like retreats and conferences.

The key is not what you do but doing so with consistency and pace. Doing all these things on a consistent basis will set things in motion and be standardized in your life as habits. This will strengthen the relationship you are building with God.

Shitsuke (Sustain)

The Sustain step ensures that 5S is applied on an ongoing basis. It is the most basic but arguably the most important. As you implement all four other S's, you need to make sure you do not lose focus on any of those steps because there will always be distractions. Sustain exists to help transform your standardized 5S processes into just the way you do things.

Once you've standardized, it's time to continually act upon those standards with a watchful eye. Sustaining the 5S methodology means focusing on maintaining the developed process with an eye focused on continuing to improve. It means that you have the green light to keep driving – kind of like a roundabout that you never leave!

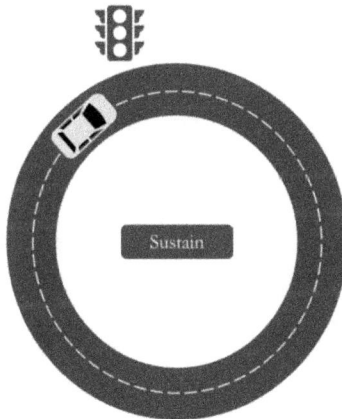

Practically speaking, it simply means going through the cycle of the previous four steps on a regular basis. As time passes, life invariably will add unwanted clutter and chaos to our lives. That's normal. Therefore, the goal is to also normalize a regular re-evaluation of Sorting, Straightening, Shining, and Standardizing.

Catch the foxes for us, the little foxes that spoil the vineyards, for our vineyards are in blossom. (Song of Solomon 2:15 ESV)

The goal of the 5S methodology is implementing a structured approach to 'catch' all the little foxes that show up in your busy life that have the potential for ruining and destroying the growth of God in your life.

CHAPTER 8

THERE'S ALWAYS MORE ROAD

Growth, like any journey, is experienced through milestones. You celebrate them—arrivals, breakthroughs, answered prayers, and healed wounds. You mark these moments with social media posts, photos, journal entries, check marks on vision boards, and many words of gratitude to a loving God. These markers are important; they remind you of how far you've come, give you hope, and fuel your faith to keep moving forward.

But no matter how far you've gone, something deep inside you knows this isn't the final destination. There's an inner whisper, a gentle tug at your heart, that says: *This isn't it. There's more.* That's because in God's unfolding story for your life, there's always more road ahead.

God, in His boundless love and infinite wisdom, continually unfolds new landscapes before you. He casts fresh vision—like a refreshed Hoshin plan—revealing deeper truths, hidden treasures, and divine purposes that you didn't see before. He gently redirects your course when you drift or get stuck, not to punish you, but to lovingly steer you back on track.

Just when you think you have "arrived," when your spirit whispers that you've reached the end of the journey, God quietly says, *There's more.* More peace beyond your current understanding. More purpose that fuels your heart. More healing that mends unseen wounds. More of Him to know, love, and reflect.

Why does God do this? Is He some hard taskmaster who is never satisfied with our efforts or labor? Absolutely not. The truth is quite the opposite. He is a loving Father who desires none of His children to perish or fall into the judgment reserved for the enemy and his schemes. His heart breaks for those who remain distant from Him, and His desire is for all to experience His mercy and grace.

If there's even a chance that just one more person could encounter His transforming love, He will do everything in His power to make that happen. And indeed, He already did—by sending His Son Jesus to the cross to bridge the gap for all humanity.

This divine love is sacred and compelling, and He calls you to carry this same passion for everyone who has yet to meet Jesus. That's why the journey never ends. There's always one more soul who needs to know the hope and salvation that can only be found in Christ. And until that happens, the road stretches onward, inviting you to move forward.

> *Therefore, go and make disciples of all the nations, baptizing them in the name of the Father and the Son and the Holy Spirit. Teach these new disciples to obey all the commands I have given you. And be sure of this: I am with you always, even to the end of the age. (Matthew 28:19-20 NLT)*

Within this book, you have been shown tools, systems, and methods to help you grow. Being honest, it's tempting to treat growth like a formula—follow the right map, use the right tools, check all the spiritual boxes, and you'll reach your destination. But this journey was never about a fixed set of methods. It's about one simple, profound truth: getting you further today than you were yesterday.

Yes, it can be difficult to sustain growth without systems and routines to support you. But spiritual growth isn't the product of a method or a formula—it's the result of a Savior.

Jesus is not a destination you arrive at and then rest. He is the companion who walks beside you every step of the way. It's not the roadmap or the tools that transform you—it's the relationship that carries you. It's not the techniques that propel you forward—it's the power of the Holy Spirit working within you.

You grow because you remain in Him, not because you've mastered a method or strategy.

> *But whatever gain I had, I counted as loss for the sake of Christ. Indeed, I count everything as loss because of the surpassing worth of knowing Christ Jesus my Lord. For his sake I have suffered the loss of all things and count them as rubbish, in order that I may gain Christ. (Philippians 3:7-8 ESV)*

Sometimes the road ahead includes long difficult miles. Sometimes you stall, take a wrong turn, or your vehicle breaks down completely. These moments can feel crushing, and you may be tempted to think you've failed or that the journey is over.

But failure is not final; it's merely a bend in the road. With the right tools and systems, you realize that it's not a dead end.

> *The LORD hears his people when they call to him*
> *for help. He rescues them from all their troubles.*
> *The LORD is close to the brokenhearted; he*
> *rescues those whose spirits are crushed. (Psalm*
> *34:17-18 NLT)*

Even in your most uncertain moments, God is not confused or disoriented. Even in your deepest struggles, He is never distant. His purpose for you remains in motion, and His presence never leaves your side. The journey continues, even when you cannot see the path clearly.

Detours don't disqualify you. Delays don't derail your destiny. The road ahead may be steep or unclear, but we move forward with confidence—not because we know every twist and turn, but because we know the One who does.

> *Jesus said to him, "I am the [only] Way [to God]*
> *and the [real] Truth and the [real] Life; no one*
> *comes to the Father but through Me. (John 14:6*
> *AMP)*

So, when you're tempted to believe your journey is finished—or that you've missed your chance—remember this: God isn't done. The work He began in you is still unfolding.

> *And I am certain that God, who began the good*
> *work within you, will continue his work until it is*
> *finally finished on the day when Christ Jesus*
> *returns. (Philippians 1:6 NLT)*

Anyone who has driven across America can testify that the open road from coast to coast will bring the traveler into forests, through desserts, onto snowcapped mountains, down to flat valleys, from cold arctics to scorching heat. In the same way, the road ahead for you may change shape. The scenery may shift. The pace may quicken or slow. But the journey continues. And with every mile, God is not just leading you forward—He's drawing you closer to Himself. This isn't the end. It's simply the next horizon.

Because in the Kingdom of God...

There's always more road.

TRACK IT!

Use these pages to document and track some of the tangible elements of your spiritual journey.

Breakthrough Goals

_____

_____

_____

_____

_____

_____

Annual Goals

_____

_____

_____

_____

_____

_____

Actions and Activities
Start:
_____

_____

_____

_____

Stop:
_____

_____

_____

_____

Continue:
_____

_____

_____

_____

Measurements
_____

_____

_____

_____

_____

Accountability
_____

_____

_____

_____

_____

Big Rocks

_____

_____

_____

_____

_____

_____

_____

_____

_____

Passengers

_____

_____

_____

_____

_____

_____

Sources Used

1. Donnelly, Darrin. "Bo Schembechler: Emphasize Execution, Not Innovation." *Sports for the Soul*, 7 Sept. 2017, sportsforthesoul.com/bo-schembechler-emphasize-execution-not-innovation/.
2. "Six Sigma Definition - What Is Lean Six Sigma? | ASQ." *Asq.org*, 2024, asq.org/quality-resources/six-sigma?srsltid=AfmBOoq_DQX2yKKskFBkQL_EVIYikTK yRbYBs49qWs5kyiUPBQzBEA_e.
3. "Six Sigma Definition - What Is Lean Six Sigma? | ASQ." *Asq.org*, 2024, asq.org/quality-resources/six-sigma?srsltid=AfmBOoq_DQX2yKKskFBkQL_EVIYikTK yRbYBs49qWs5kyiUPBQzBEA_e.
4. Jacobson, Greg. "The Meaning of Hoshin Kanri: What, Why, and How." *Kainexus.com*, 2019, blog.kainexus.com/improvement-disciplines/hoshin-kanri/hoshin-kanri-what-why-and-how.
5. Becher, Jonathan. "Prioritize the Big Rocks." *Manage by Walking Around*, 5 May 2024, jonathanbecher.com/2024/05/05/prioritize-the-big-rocks/.
6. "Poka-Yoke." *Six Sigma Daily*, 5 Feb. 2022, www.sixsigmadaily.com/poka-yoke/.
7. Costa, Ines. "The Ultimate Guide to 5S and 5S Training | KAIZEN™ Article." *Kaizen.com*, 24 May 2024, kaizen.com/insights/ultimate-guide-5s-training/.
8. "About the KonMari Method – KonMari | the Official Website of Marie Kondo." *KonMari | the Official Website of Marie Kondo*, 2 Feb. 2022, konmari.com/about-the-konmari-method/?srsltid=AfmBOoqbepoQn6kBe0RT1Atp9Lx6felcm D5Ivv7y34mL68e8PBE7xLsa.